# GREAT BEERS

## 700 OF THE BEST FROM AROUND THE WORLD

EDITOR-IN-CHIEF **TIM HAMPSON**

**Project Editor** Robert Sharman
**Project Art Editor** Nihal Yesil
**Designer** Elma Aquino
**Managing Editor** Dawn Henderson
**Managing Art Editors** Christine Keilty, Marianne Markham
**DTP Designers** Harish Aggarwal, Pushpak Tyagi
**DTP Manager** Sunil Sharma
**Production Manager, DK India** Pankaj Sharma
**Editorial Manager, DK India** Glenda Fernandes
**Senior Jacket Designer** Vanessa Hamilton
**Producer, Pre-Production** Robert Dunn
**Producer** Naomi Green
**Creative Technical Support** Sonia Charbonnier
**Special Sales Creative Project Manager** Alison Donovan

Content first published in Great Britain in 2008
in *The Beer Book*
This edition first published in 2010
by Dorling Kindersley Limited
80 Strand, London WC2R 0RL

Copyright © 2008, 2010, 2017 Dorling Kindersley Limited
A Penguin Random House Company
2 4 6 8 10 9 7 5 3 1
001-176112-Sept/2017

A CIP catalogue record for this book is available from
the British Library.
ISBN 978-0-2413-2398-4

Colour reproduction by Colourscan, Singapore
Printed and bound in China

A WORLD OF IDEAS
SEE ALL THERE IS TO KNOW
www.dk.com

# Contents

# Introduction

This book is an adventure – a journey through a fascinating world of flavours, colours, and aromas. These pages constitute a trip around the world in 700 ales, porters, and pilsners, and an introduction to the master brewers behind the world's greatest drink.

These are exciting times for beer lovers. With the USA leading the way in terms of innovation, in the last few decades brewers have been pushing at boundaries as never before. From Alaska to the Mexican border, America's craft brewers are brewing darker beers, bitterer beers, and hoppier beers than can be found anywhere else in the world. European beer styles are being taken apart and put back together with barely a nod to tradition. In brewing terms, there are simply no rules anymore.

Meanwhile, the great brewing nations of Europe – Germany, Belgium, the Czech Republic – still stand tall, with glorious tradition standing alongside intriguing innovation. Countries historically associated more with grape than grain are also making great strides – Italy's brewers are among the most experimental and ambitious worldwide, and their efforts have been yielding remarkable results.

The other good news for lovers of great beer is that it has never been easier for drinkers to sample such a wide range of beers from around the world. A trip to your local shop or supermarket will in most cases provide a selection of several of the brews featured in this book. More ambitious readers may be encouraged to travel further to track down exciting tipples and experience the brewing and drinking culture of some of the world's top beer destinations. If this appeals to you, this book introduces tours of Oregon, Brussels, the Cotswolds, Prague, and Bamberg – a range of destinations representing the best of the old and new worlds of beer.

This book is intended for people who want to broaden their knowledge of beer and hunt down exciting brews from around the globe. It should encourage you never to ask just for a beer without first considering its style – pilsner or wheat, fruit or an American IPA, Belgian ale or a gueuze? For there can be few better pleasures – when returning home after a long day at work or just sitting in a favourite bar – than the pleasure of a great beer. But which one? The choice is yours – enjoy the experience.

Tim Hampson

# Aass Bryggeri

Postboks 1530,
N-3007 Drammen, **NORWAY**
www.aass.no

Norway's oldest brewery dates
back to 1834. Named after Poul
Lauritz Aass (pronounced
"ouse"), it is a family-owned
business run by four generations
since 1860.

**BREWING SECRET** Aass brews
according to the strict 1516 Bavarian Law
of Purity, drawing its water from
the nearby lake of Glitre.

## Aass Bock

DUNKLER BOCK **6.5%** ABV
Smooth and creamy; brewed using
Munich malt and Hallertau hops. Lagered
for at least three months.

## Aass Juleøl

DUNKLER BOCK **6.2%** ABV
The most sought-after Christmas beer
in Scandinavia. Thick and malty with
a smooth, rich flavour.

# Abbaye des Rocs

37, Chaussée Brunehault, B7387
Montignies-sur-Roc, **BELGIUM**
www.abbaye-des-rocs.com

Jean-Pierre Eloir, a former
exciseman, took up brewing
in 1979. The business has since
expanded, with the beers gaining
a good reputation, particularly
abroad, and some are now being
developed with export in mind.

**BREWING SECRET** Core beers are true
to the spiced and well-bodied Walloon
style; keg beers are often unfiltered.

### Blanche des Honnelles

**WITBIER 6% ABV**
Not your usual wheat beer, this one is
made from malted barley, malted wheat,
and home-malted oats.

### Abbaye des Rocs Brune

**BELGIAN DARK STRONG ALE 9% ABV**
Very spiced and sustaining, with
a nourishing touch. Well-liked in Anglo-
Saxon countries.

# Achelse Kluis

De Kluis 1, B3930 Hamont-Achel,
**BELGIUM**
www.achelsekluis.org

At a time when there were many
brewery closures, the Belgian
beer world had cause to celebrate
in 1998. That was when De
Achelse Kluis – a Trappist abbey
on the Dutch border – started
up brewing again after 84
unproductive years! It is run as a
pub-brewery, and draws in many
passing walkers and cyclists.

### Achel Bruin 8

TRAPPIST BEER 8% ABV
More than the draft beers on tap, this
is a classic Trappist brew; heavy, estery,
and filling.

### Achel Extra Bruin

DARK TRAPPIST 9.5% ABV
The flagship of brewmaster Knops – who
refuses to drink anything else – rich
and rewarding.

# Acorn

Wombwell, Barnsley,
South Yorkshire, S73 8HA
**ENGLAND**
www.acornbrewery.net

One of the newer microbreweries
in England, Acorn was set up
in 2003 and doubled capacity
in its first four years. It now
produces 40 barrels (6,500 litres)
every week.

**BREWING SECRET** The yeast strain
from the 1850s Barnsley Brewery has
been reintroduced, coinciding with the
company gathering significant awards.

## Barnsley Bitter

BITTER **3.8**% ABV
Ripe chestnut in colour, with a
rounded, rich flavour that lingers
in the bitter finish.

## Barnsley Gold

STRONG BITTER **4.3**% ABV
Beautifully golden, with citrus fruit
hop aromas orchestrating the ensemble
through to its dry finish.

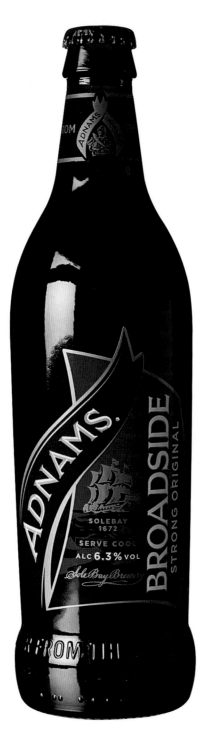

# Adnams

Southwold, Suffolk, IP18 6JW
**ENGLAND**
www.adnams.co.uk

Its "Beers from the Coast" have been brewed in the classic English seaside town of Southwold since 1872. In recent years, technological innovation has driven refurbishment, while an emphasis on traditional methods has been studiously maintained. An eco-friendly distribution centre – complete with living grass roof – summarizes the dynamic approach.

### Adnams Broadside
STRONG BITTER **4.7**% ABV
Rich, fruitcake aromas dominate initially, giving way to an elegant hop and malt association.

### Adnams Bitter
BITTER **3.7**% ABV
Aromatic hop and biscuit malt fragrances introduce a lingering, dry, and refreshingly bitter flavour.

# Airbräu

Münchner Airportcenter,
Terminalstr. Mitte 18, 85356
München, **GERMANY**
www.allresto.de

This brewery has a unique
location: set between the two
terminals of Munich airport. It
opened in 2004 at the same time
as the airport's new Terminal 2,
and it includes a much-
frequented restaurant and
beer garden. Two brewing
kettles are situated right in
the middle of the restaurant.

### Fliegerquell
**LAGER 5.2% ABV**
Deep golden, finely structured,
and classically dry. It is brewed
for international palates.

### Kumulus
**WHITE BEER 5.4% ABV**
Typical yellow colour; a sparkling,
very fresh white beer, refreshing
and full-bodied.

# Aktien

Hohe Buchleute 3, 87600
Kaufbeuren, **GERMANY**
www.aktienbrauerei.de

The origins of brewing at the
Aktien brewery in Kaufbeuren
can be traced back to the early
14th century. In more recent
times, Aktien has taken over the
Löwen and Rosen breweries.

**BREWING SECRET** Aktien still brews
its beer strictly according to the Bavarian
Purity Law set in 1516.

## Naturtrübes Kellerbier
**KELLERBIER 5.1% ABV**
Unfiltered and naturally cloudy
out of the cellar. The slightly sweet taste
is typical of one of the oldest styles of
beer in Bavaria.

## Fendt Dieselrossöl
**MÄRZEN 5.9% ABV**
A malty, aromatic structure and
a full-bodied, slightly bitter taste.
Goes well with venison dishes.

# Alaskan

5429 Shaune Drive, Juneau,
Alaska 99801, **USA**
www.alaskanbeer.com

Although it is located in a coastal
community without roads
connecting it to the rest of the
United States, Alaskan Brewing
has grown into a regional force,
selling its beer over much of the
nation west of the Rockies.
Founders Geoff and Marcy
Larson focused on native
ingredients and recipes from
the outset. Alaskan's Amber Ale,
is based on a beer made across
the channel from Juneau at the
turn of the 20th century.

### Amber
ALTBIER 5% ABV
Clean caramel on the nose, brightened
by spicy hops. Smooth and malty, with
balanced bitterness.

### Barley Wine Ale
BARLEY WINE 10.4% ABV
Cellared in a former gold mine. Rich and
smooth, with dark caramel, cherries,
and plums. Nicely balanced.

# A. Le Coq

Tähtvere 56/62, 50050 Tartu,
**ESTONIA**
www.alecoq.ee/en

This brewery was founded in
1826, and purchased in 1913
by A. Le Coq, a London-based
company. At the time, it was
looking for a brewery in the
Russian Empire where it could
produce its Imperial Stout rather
than export it from England.
Production was halted in the
1960s but revived in 1999.
A small museum is housed
in the former maltings.

### Le Coq Porter
PORTER **6.5%** ABV
A strong, dark beer – a worthy
successor to the famous Imperial
Extra Double Stout.

### Double Bock
BOCK **8%** ABV
A strong and warming light bock,
it has a surprisingly mellow finish
for a beer of this strength.

# Alesmith

9368 Cabot Drive, San Diego,
California 92126, **USA**
www.alesmith.com

One of several San Diego
breweries that has pushed
Southern California to the
forefront of national brewing.
It has a wide following for its
mostly strong and often esoteric
beers, many barrel-aged and
vintage-dated.

**BREWING SECRET** Every employee
is an award-winning home brewer.

## Speedway Stout
IMPERIAL STOUT **12% ABV**
It's coffee-infused, complementing
a broad imperial palate of chocolate,
toffee, currants, and oily nuts.

## IPA
INDIA PALE ALE **7.3% ABV**
Brimming with hops and fruit salad
aromas, including notes of ripe mango
and pineapple.

# Alhambra

Avenida de Murcia 1,
18012 Granada, **SPAIN**
www.cervezasalhambra.com

The Alhambra group was founded in 1925 and is named after Granada's famed Moorish palace. Spain's purest water comes from the nearby Sierra Nevada mountain range, and is used in the making of Alhambra beers.

**BREWING SECRET** The brewery uses traditional techniques that include fermentation lasting up to 39 days.

### Alhambra Premium
LAGER 4.6% ABV
A soft gold in colour, its nose is lemony and fresh with a hint of malt. A well-balanced quaffable beer.

### Mezquita
WHEAT BEER 7.2% ABV
A full-bodied, assertive red wheat beer with caramel notes and hints of pepper in the aroma.

# Allagash

100 Industrial Way, Portland,
Maine 04103, **USA**
www.allagash.com

Focusing on Belgian-inspired
beers, Allagash draws on
tradition but does not shy away
from innovation. In 2007 it
became the first American
brewery to build a traditional
"coolship" (a huge, open,
shallow pan) for spontaneous
fermentation by wild yeasts.

**BREWING SECRET** Some speciality
beers are aged in oak bourbon barrels.

## Allagash White
WITBIER 6.2% ABV
Appropriately cloudy, fruity, and
refreshing. Brightened by subtle
coriander and Curaçao orange peel.

## Curieux
TRIPLE 10% ABV
Allagash Tripel ale, aged in Jim Beam
barrels. Orchard fruits and honey meet
bourbon, vanilla, and wood.

# Allersheim

Allersheim 6,
37603 Holzminden, **GERMANY**
www.brauerei-allersheim.de

Founded in 1854, this brewery was, for Otto Baumgarten, merely a sideline to farming. He harvested the grain in his own fields, but had to buy in the hops. Production grew over the years, though, and today the brewery has 40 employees.

**BREWING SECRET** The beers are brewed to suit discerning local palates.

## Landbier
PILSNER 5% ABV
A pilsner with a mash bill from light and dark malt. Soft in taste, with a typical malty aroma.

## Blue Moon
BEER AND COLA 1.9% ABV
A pleasant mix of dry hops and cola. It's not too sweet, because the mix is produced without sugar.

# Almond 22

Via Dietro le Mura 36/38,
65010 Spoltore (PE), **ITALY**
www.birraalmond.com

This microbrewery was founded
in 2003, in the seaside town of
Pescara, by Swedish-Italian Jurij
Ferri. He brews highly praised
ales inspired by British and
Belgian styles, as well as some
original, experimental beers that
use local ingredients.

### Torbata
BARLEY WINE 8.7% ABV
Peated ale with a smoky flavour similar
to a Scotch whisky. Easy to drink despite
its strength.

### Farrotta
SPELT WHEAT ALE 5.7% ABV
Cloudy golden ale brewed using
barley and locally grown spelt; easy-
drinking and thirst-quenching.

# Alpirsbach

Alpirsbacher Klosterbräu,
Marktplatz 1, 72275 Alpirsbach,
**GERMANY**
www.alpirsbacher.de

A railway was constructed through the Black Forest at the end of the 19th century, which brought many visitors to the village of Alpirsbach. Johann Gottfried Glauner helped to cater for them by reopening the old village brewery. Sales were good, and today the beer from Alpirsbach is produced by the fourth generation of the family.

### Kleiner Mönch

LAGER 5.2% ABV

The golden colour promises a fresh, young beer. It is full-bodied with a flavour of caramel from the malt.

### Schwarzes Pils

PILSNER 4.9% ABV

Deep red-black colour and a strong taste, with a roasted malt aroma that is unmistakable.

# Altöttinger

Altöttinger Hell-Brau,
Herrenmühlstr. 15, 84503 Altötting,
**GERMANY**
www.altoettinger-hellbraeu.de

The Bavarian town of Altötting is
home to the Altötting Madonna, a
world-famous pilgrimage site. In
1890 Georg Hell expanded
production at a local brewery to
help cater to thirsty pilgrims.
Today the brewery produces
eight different beers.

**BREWING SECRET** The finest hops and
best German malts are used.

## Bayerische Dunkel
DUNKEL 5.2% ABV
Roasty and malty taste, but fresh, and
with a long finish. A dark speciality with
its own character.

## Fein-Herb
LAGER 5% ABV
The best malts, combined with a
careful selection of hops, produce an
exceptionally dry, fine taste.

# Amber

Bielkówko, ul. Gregorkiewicza 1,
83-050 Kolbud, **POLAND**
www.browar-amber.pl

Owned by the Przybylo family,
this medium-sized brewery is one
of the most modern in Poland.
Situated close to Gdansk in
Pomerania, an area with a rich
brewing tradition, the brewery
is a supporter of the Slow Food
movement, and organizes the
Kozlaki Bielkowskie food and
drink festival every September.

### Koźlak
DUNKEL BOCK **6.5**% ABV
A ruby-red beer, it is rich in malt
and yeasty flavours, with a warming
aftertaste.

### Zywe
PILSNER **6.2**% ABV
Pale in colour, it has lemon flavours
and uses hops and barley from the
Lubin region.

# Amsterdam Brewing

21 Bathurst Street, Toronto,
Ontario, M5V 2NG, **CANADA**
www.amsterdambeer.com

Purity, passion, and revelry are the watchwords for Toronto's first brewpub. Founded in 1986, it was an immediate success. Business was brisk, and it soon moved to another site before finding its current home in 2005. The brewery stands opposite the historic Fort York, the 1793 birthplace of modern Toronto. In 2003, when the Kawartha Lakes Brewing Company closed, its brands were sold to Amsterdam Brewing.

## KLB Nut Brown Ale

BROWN ALE 5% ABV

The unmistakable tang of East Kent Golding hops. Sweet to taste, it has hints of honey and chocolate.

## Amsterdam Wheat Beer

WHEAT BEER 4% ABV

Light in colour, with malt sweetness and a hint of fresh bread. Often served chilled with a slice of lemon.

# Anchor

705 Mariposa St., San Francisco,
California 94107, **USA**
www.anchorbrewing.com

Fritz Maytag saved Anchor
Brewing from closing in 1965,
introduced US drinkers to many
classic styles, and launched a
microbrewery revolution.

**BREWING SECRET** Maytag is known for
preserving the USA's indigenous "steam
style", which involves using bottom-
fermenting yeast at high temperatures
in wide, shallow, open pans.

## Liberty Ale
PALE ALE 6% ABV
A benchmark American pale ale. Fruity
and floral on the nose; crisp bitterness on
the palate.

## Anchor Steam
STEAM BEER 4.9% ABV
A signature woody, minty nose. Well-
rounded caramel flavours yield to a firm,
crisp finish.

# Andechs

Kloster Andechs, Bergstr. 2,
82346 Andechs, **GERMANY**
www.andechs.de

The Benedictine monks of
Andechs began to produce beer
in 1455. The monastery updated
its brewery in 1972, investing in
modern equipment. Still closely
associated with the holy
mountain pilgrimage site
southwest of Munich, Andechs
today is a brand name that's
internationally known.

### Bergbock Hell
BOCK 7% ABV
A strong beer, but it tastes mild and
aromatic. Its typical light sweetness
gives it a full body.

### Doppelbock Dunkel
BOCK 7% ABV
This world-famous beer has a really
strong taste. The dark malts give it an
unmistakable character, with a light
aroma of hops in the finish.

# Anderson Valley

17700 Highway 253, Boonville,
California 95415, **USA**
www.avbc.com

Set in Mendocino County's
picturesque Anderson Valley,
this solar-powered brewery
mixes local and international
styles and techniques. Some
beer names are those of local
landmarks, others are in
Boontling, a regional dialect.

**BREWING SECRET** The copper brew
kettles were rescued from a closed-down
German brewery.

## Boont ESB
EXTRA SPECIAL BITTER **6.8**% ABV
Citrusy hops layer fruit on top of bready
malt. Tangy in the middle; a long and
mildly bitter finish.

## Barney Flats Oatmeal Stout
OATMEAL STOUT **5.7**% ABV
Impression of coffee and cream,
sweetness balanced by roasted grains,
the complexity heightened by earthy
undertones.

# Anheuser-Busch

One Busch Place, St. Louis,
Missouri 63118, **USA**
www.anheuser-busch.com

Anheuser-Busch brews half the
beer sold in the United States,
including Budweiser and Bud
Light, two of the world's best-
selling brands. With its Michelob
line, seasonal specialities,
and beers produced by its
regional breweries for local
consumers, the company has
significantly broadened the
range of its beers.

## Michelob
MALT LAGER 5% ABV
Returned to its all-malt roots in 2007.
Delicate, with a spicy nose, clean malt
middle and crisp, dry finish.

## Stone Mill Organic Pale Ale
PALE ALE 5.5% ABV
Organic beer under the Green Valley
Brewing label. This ale is lightly bready
with earthy hop character.

# Anker

Guido Gezellelaan 49,
B2800 Mechelen, **BELGIUM**
www.hetanker.be

Now here's a brewery with a
history. The owners claim it
began in 1369, but it was in 1873
that the Van Breedam family
took over and began its modern
brewing age. In the 1990s, the
end for the classic Gouden
Carolus seemed near, but a
family buy-out from the ill-fated
RIVA empire succeeded, and now
the brewery is productive and
innovative once more.

### Gouden Carolus Classic

STRONG DARK ALE 8.5% ABV
This malt bomb has a characteristic taste
of raisins in portwine. An exemplary
strong dark Belgian ale.

### Gouden Carolus Christmas

STRONG DARK ALE 10.5% ABV
The raisins and molasses from
the Carolus Classic are present,
but with a greater alcohol kick.

# Ankerbräu Nordlingen

Ankergasse 4, 86720 Nördlingen,
**GERMANY**
www.ankerbrauerei.de

The brewery's history can be traced from 1608, when several beers were brewed here for a festival. It was acquired by the Grandel family at the end of the 19th century.

**BREWING SECRET** The beers are made with local malts, mineral water from the Ries, and hops from Spalt.

### Lager Hell
LAGER 5% ABV

A full-flavoured clear, yellow beer; pleasant and full-bodied, with a fine aroma at the beginning.

### Nördlinger Premium Pils
PILSNER 4.7% ABV

A very flowery hop aroma turns slightly bitter and a bit sparkling on the tongue.

# Antares

17 Esquina 71, La Plata - P de Bs As, 7600, **ARGENTINA**
www.cervezaantares.com.ar

Antares is the brightest star in the Scorpius constellation, and the brewpub that shares its name sparkles too. Stylish and smart, it offers a lively alternative to beers from international brewers. Brews include a kölsch, a Scotch ale, a honey beer, a cream stout, a barley wine, and an imperial stout, with some variations in style.

## Antares Kölsch
KÖLSCH 5% ABV
A well hopped and highly drinkable ale style. Good fruity overtones make it an ideal partner to food.

## Antares Stout Imperial
IMPERIAL STOUT 8.5% ABV
Intense liquorice and toasted flavours give way to roasted coffee and caramelized orange intensities.

# Apatinska Pivara

Trg Oslobodenja 5, Apatin,
25260, **SERBIA**
www.inbev.com

The biggest brewer in Serbia
and the largest in the Balkans,
this InBev-owned company now
has 46 per cent of the local
market. The town of Apatini,
which is on the Danube, is in
a fertile barley-growing area
called Vojvodina. Records show
that brewing has taken place
in the town since 1756.

### Jelen Pivo

LAGER 5% ABV
Light yellow in colour, with a white,
wispy head. It has hints of grass and
grain and aromas of hops and malt.
*Jelen* means "deer".

### Apatinsko Pivo

LAGER 5% ABV
A fresh-tasting beer with floral notes
and a citrus aroma.

# Arcadia

103 West Michigan Avenue,
Battle Creek, Michigan 49017, **USA**
www.arcadiabrewingcompany.com

Using the British Peter Austin
system more common in the
Northeast, and brewing with
British malts, Arcadia leans
toward UK-inspired ales, but
made with citrusy and piney
Pacific Northwest hops.
Ringwood yeast gives the beers
a fresh character, and they work
particularly well on cask.

### London Porter

PORTER **7.2%** ABV
Rich on the nose, flavours of coffee
beans, chocolate, and dark fruit, with
a lingering, dessert-like finish.

### Scotch Ale

SCOTTISH ALE **7.5%** ABV
Nuttiness and piney hops don't totally
balance here. The final impression is
of sweet caramel.

# Arco

Schlossallee 1, 94554 Moos,
**GERMANY**
www.arcobraeu.de

Arco has been owned by the
Counts of Arco-Zinneberg for
450 years. The castle and
brewery belonging to the family
are situated in Moos, a small
town in the heart of Niederbayern
in Bavaria, where the rivers Isar
and Donau converge. The current
Count Arco personally launched
the beers in the USA in 2004.

## Schloss Hell

LAGER **4.9**% ABV

With its soft but full-bodied taste and
golden colour, Arco's Schloss Hell typifies
Bavarian lager.

## Urfass

LAGER **5.2**% ABV

Slightly more bitter than the Schloss Hell,
and especially spicy, this is a real
premium lager of Bavaria.

# Asia Pacific Breweries

459 Jalan Ahmad Ibrahim,
639934 **SINGAPORE**
www.tigerbeer.com

Widely available across Asia, AP's beers are now brewed in seven different countries. Tiger Beer – its most famous – was first produced in the 1930s, when the "Time for a Tiger" slogan was first used. Anthony Burgess named the first novel in his The Long Day Wanes trilogy *Time for a Tiger*.

### Tiger
LAGER 5% ABV
A golden coloured refreshing lager. It is normally served so chilled that its taste and aromas are masked.

### ABC Extra Stout
STOUT 8% ABV
A strong but easy-drinking beer. The nose is robust, with roasted coffee and chocolate flavours.

# Auer

Münchner Str. 80, 83022 Rosenheim,
**GERMANY**
www.auerbraeu.de

Between 1887 and 1920, Johann
Auer acquired several plots
of land and some breweries
around the town of Rosenheim,
southeast of Munich. Since
then, the company has
expanded considerably.

**BREWING SECRET** When it was
founded, this was one of the most
modern breweries in Bavaria.

### Bajuware Dunkel
**DUNKEL 5.5% ABV**
Brewed in old-fashioned Bavarian style,
this beer has a malty aroma and a
full-bodied character.

### Weizenbock
**WHEAT BOCK 7% ABV**
A strong, spicy speciality. A good
accompaniment to hearty cheeses
or sweet desserts.

# Augustiner

Landsberger Str. 31-35, 80339
München, **GERMANY**
www.augustiner-braeu.de

Founded in 1328, this is the oldest brewery in Munich and one of only two in the city (along with Hofbräu München) that do not belong to a giant of the global brewing industry. The site as it is today was constructed in 1885. Augustiner beer has become famous around the world even though the brewery does not advertise itself.

### Edelstoff
EXPORT **5.6**% ABV
The unusual dark golden colour displays its special character. A sweet and obvious hop taste guides you to a very malty finish.

### Weissbier
WHEAT BEER **5.4**% ABV
Golden and cloudy, this is a full-bodied wheat beer with a citrus taste and light bitters in the finish.

# August Schell

1860 Schell Road, New Ulm,
Minnesota 56073, **USA**
www.schellsbrewery.com

Family-owned since August
Schell founded it in 1860, this
brewery has perhaps the most
beautiful setting in the USA,
with ornamental gardens and a
former carriage house converted
into a museum. In 2002 the
company took over production
of the legendary Grain Belt
Premium beer, when that
brewery failed, to save a
Minnesota icon from extinction.

### Caramel Bock

BOCK 5.6% ABV
Rich caramel on the nose, turning
rummy on the palate. Sweetness
lingers after a not-quite dry finish.

### Schmaltz Alt

ALTBIER 5% ABV
Subtle combination of biscuit and
chocolate balanced by mild, slightly
spicy hop flavours and bitterness.

# Au in der Hallertau

Schlossbrauerei Au in der Hallertau,
Schlossbräugasse 2, 84072 Au,
**GERMANY**
www.auer-bier.de

Au is at the heart of the largest
hop-growing area in the world.
It was linked with the master
brewer Schweiger in 1590 and,
since 1846, has been owned by
six generations of the Earls
Beck of Peccoz. A modern
approach is an essential feature
of the management at Au in
der Hallertau.

### Hopfengold
**EXPORT 5% ABV**
Golden colour, full-bodied taste with fine
bitters of hops and clear malt. Nice finish,
not too sweet.

### Holledauer Leichtes
**WHEAT BEER 3.3% ABV**
A cloudy yellow, light wheat beer, fresh
and lightly sparkling; not too heavy a
taste, and with a slightly bitter finish.

# Avery

5763 Arapahoe Avenue, Boulder,
Colorado 80803, **USA**
www.averybrewing.com

Located near the Rocky
Mountains, though in a
nondescript industrial park,
this brewery has earned a
reputation for its hoppy beers
and its astonishingly strong
beers (sometimes they are both).
These include a threesome
nicknamed the "Demons of Ale",
in which the beers average
15 per cent ABV apiece.

### India Pale Ale

INDIA PALE ALE **6.3**% ABV
Piney, oily nose, with grapefruit and
orange from the aroma to the palate.
Unapologetically bitter.

### Salvation

BELGIAN STRONG GOLDEN ALE **9**% ABV
Fleshy fruits, particularly apricots,
mingle with sweet, spicy aromas and
flavours, and a surprising hint of honey.

# Ayinger

Zornedinger Str. 1, 85653 Aying,
**GERMANY**
www.ayinger.de

Johann Liebhard founded this
brewery in Aying in 1876, at
a time when there were about
6,000 breweries in Bavaria.
That number has dropped to
about 700 today, but Ayinger
has survived and was renovated
by the Inselkammer family in
1999. It has since become more
widely known.

### Jahrhundertbier

EXPORT 5.5% ABV

A honey-like aroma with light flowery
hops leads on to a harmonious finish.

### Celebrator

DOPPELBOCK 6.7% ABV

The taste of malt dominates this nearly
black, strong beer. It is not as sweet as
other doppelbocks of the same quality.

# Baird Brewing

9-4 Senbonminato-cho, Numazu City,
Shizuoka 410-0845, **JAPAN**
www.bairdbeer.com

Founded by Ohio native Bryan
Baird and his wife Sayuri in
January 2001, Baird has come
to be considered Japan's best
brewery. After the six regular
beers were established – later
augmented by an American-style
wheat ale – Baird then focused on
many seasonal beers. The Bairds
have recently opened a taproom
in Tokyo.

### Rising Sun Pale Ale

PALE ALE **5**% ABV

A brilliant American-style Pale Ale made
with British Maris Otter malt and with
a unique US hop signature.

### Angry Boy Brown Ale

BROWN ALE **6.2**% ABV

Exciting and complex, this strong brown
ale has a complex flavour profile and
a richly satisfying finish.

# Le Baladin

Piazza V Luglio 15,
12060 Piozzo (CN), **ITALY**
www.birreria.com

Charismatic, pioneering Teo Musso is internationally known as one of the most creative brewers in the world. He has turned beer into a type of wine and created beer truffles – not even he knows what he will do next.

**BREWING SECRET** Musso plays music to his yeasts during the fermentation process, believing that they respond.

## Xyauyù
**BARLEY WINE 12% ABV**
Radical oxidization gives "solera" sherry-like favours. A flat, warming, velvety nightcap. A masterpiece.

## Nora
**SPICED ALE 6.8% ABV**
Inspired by ancient Egypt, using kamut grains, ginger, and myrrh. A balsamic bitterness comes from Ethiopian resins.

# Baltika

6 Proezd, Parnas 4,
St Petersburg, **RUSSIA**
www.eng.baltika.ru

The Russian beer market has been going through a period of rapid change as it continues to adjust to a capitalist economy. Baltika's rise has been swift, and it is now the country's largest beer producer. It brews the top two brands – Baltika and Arsenalnoye. The company accounts for more than seven out of ten beer sales, and exports to 46 countries.

### Baltika No 3 Classic
LAGER 4.8% ABV
A malty nose gives way to a bitter finish. Widely available across Russia.

### Baltika No 6 Porter
PORTER 7% ABV
A well-balanced beer. Dark roasted malts, chocolate and molasses flavours fill the glass, overlayed by a good hop finish.

# Barley

Via C. Colombo, 09040
Maracalagonis (CA), Sardinia, **ITALY**
www.barley.it

Skilful home brewer Nicola Perra established this microbrewery in 2006 in southern Sardinia, challenging the mass-market lagers so popular in the region (consumption here is the highest in Italy).

**BREWING SECRET** Local ingredients such as Sardinian wine wort and organic honey are used in the ales.

## Toccadibò

GOLDEN STRONG ALE **8.4%** ABV
A warming ale; spicy, hoppy and dry, with intriguing bitter-almond notes of amaretto.

## BB 10

BARLEY WINE **10%** ABV
A unique brew made with sapa, the boiled wort of local Cannonau grapes. A highly distinctive nightcap.

# Barons

1 Moncur Street, Woollahra,
New South Wales 2025, **AUSTRALIA**
www.baronsbrewing.com

"Beer barons" by name and nature, this relative newcomer has its brands produced under contract and is one of the country's fastest-growing craft beer players; they are also eyeing export markets in Russia and the USA.

**BREWING SECRET** Barons makes use of indigenous "bush tucker" ingredients, such as wattle seed and lemon myrtle.

## Lemon Myrtle Witbier

BELGIAN WITBIER 5% ABV
Moderate carbonation, lime-scented mid-palate with spicy hints, followed by a clean, crisp finish.

## Black Wattle Original Ale

SPICED AMBER ALE 5.8% ABV
Creamy mouthfeel, malt-driven, with hints of roasted nuts, chocolate, and milky coffee.

# Bateman

Wainfleet, Lincolnshire,
PE24 4JE **ENGLAND**
www.bateman.co.uk

One of the country's oldest
and most picturesque family
breweries – with a windmill
towering high above – it has
a well-deserved reputation for
"good honest ales". A family
split almost destroyed the
business in the 1980s, but it
survived, blossomed, and has
developed a new brewhouse
and engaging visitor centre.

### Batemans XXXB

STRONG BITTER **4.8**% ABV
Classic russet-tan ale, with a well
constructed blend of malt, hops,
and fruitiness.

### XB Bitter

BITTER **3.7**% ABV
Finely balanced, with an apple-influenced
hop aroma that lingers alongside the
malty flavour.

# Bath Ales

Warmley, Bristol,
BS30 8XN **ENGLAND**
www.bathales.com

The founders' brewing backgrounds and insistence on traditional methods operating alongside cutting-edge technology has resulted in Bath Ale's reputation for distinctive, characterful, and flavoursome ales. The success of the business has led to the brewery twice outgrowing its premises since it was established in 1995. A bottling plant and shop continue the growth.

### Bath Ales Gem

BEST BITTER **4.1%** ABV
Rich and full-textured, with a malt, fruit, and bitter-sweet hop quality throughout.

### Special Pale Ale (SPA)

PALE ALE **3.7%** ABV
A prominent hop aroma and bitter malty touch complement its light-bodied character.

# Bathams

Brierley Hill, West Midlands,
DY5 2TN **ENGLAND**
www.bathams.com

The brewery's frontage –
actually the Vine Inn – is
emblazoned with a quotation
from Shakespeare's *Two
Gentlemen of Verona*: "Blessing
of you: You brew good ale". Five
generations of the Batham family
have been involved since the
brewery was established in 1877,
each nurturing its reputation for
classic Black Country mild ales.

## Bathams Best Bitter

BEST BITTER **4.5% ABV**
Straw-coloured ale, with an initial
sweetness, soon overtaken by a complex,
dry, hoppy flavour.

## Bathams Mild Ale

MILD **3.5% ABV**
A fruity, dark brown mild; sweet
and well-balanced, with a hoppy
fruit finish.

# Bavik

Rijksweg 33, B8531 Bavikhove –
Harelbeke, **BELGIUM**
www.bavik.be

With the fourth generation of
the De Brabandere family, this
brewery is run efficiently and
encompasses a large number
of tied pubs too.

**BREWING SECRET** Abbey ales and
pilsners form an important role in
the annual output (especially to
supermarkets), but the most interesting
brews are in the oud bruin tradition.

## Petrus Oud Bruin (Dark)
OUD BRUIN **5.5%** ABV
Recently, the brewery invested in giant
wooden barrels for fermenting this
vinous, quite traditional ale.

## Petrus Aged Pale
OUD BRUIN **7.3%** ABV
In the new barrels, you'll find this: the
undiluted pale beer, ageing for years,
gaining sourish, fruity notes.

# Bayern Meister Bier

1254-1 Kawaharabata, Inouede-aza, Fujinomiya City, Shizuoka 418-0103, **JAPAN**
www.bmbier.com

Brewmaster Stefan Rager originally came to Japan to brew at several start-up microbreweries which opened after the 1995 liberalization. Later, with his Japanese wife, he founded a boutique-style brewery dedicated to German beer styles. The German Embassy in Tokyo is one of his most loyal customers.

### Prinz Pils

PILSNER 5.5% ABV
Pale yellow, soft mouthfeel with low carbonation. The subtle flavours are in excellent balance.

### Amadeus Doppelbock

DOPPELBOCK 8% ABV
Very deep reddish brown, with coffee, toffee, and caramel aromas. Rich tangy malt and high alcohol suggest rum-soaked fruitcake.

# Bear Republic

345 Healdsburg Avenue, Healdsburg,
California 95448, **USA**
www.bearrepublic.com

With a brewpub located amidst
the Sonoma County wine-tasting
rooms and a brewery north of
town, Bear Republic presents
a decidedly different break
for wine tourists. Founding
brewmaster (and fireman and
race-car-driver) Richard
Norgrove is just as skilled as
any wine blender when merging
hops flavours and aromas.

## Racer 5

INDIA PALE ALE 7% ABV
Delightfully fresh grapefruit and thick
piney aromas, built on a resinous,
malty-sweet middle.

## Hop Rod Rye

IMPERIAL INDIA PALE ALE 8% ABV
Bright, citrusy nose with spicy alcohols.
A subtle blend of biscuit and clean rye.
Incessant hops.

# Beba

Viale Italia 11,
10069 Villar Perosa (TO), **ITALY**
www.birrabeba.it

Pioneering brothers Alessandro
and Enrico Borio brew a wide
range of regular and seasonal
lagers at their microbrewery
founded in 1996 near Turin.
The adjoining tap-room serves
all the house beers on draught
along with excellent food.
The local speciality is *gofri*, a
crisp unleavened bread stuffed
with cheeses, cured meats
or preserves.

### Motor Oil

STRONG DARK LAGER **8%** ABV
Ebony-coloured, with strong notes
of liquorice and roasted coffee, beans
and a long, bitter finish. As viscous
as its namesake.

### Talco

RYE LAGER **4.2%** ABV
Seasonal "rye weizen-lager" is a
thirst-quenching treat on a hot
summer afternoon.

# Bell's

8938 Krum Avenue, Galesburg,
Michigan 49053, **USA**
www.bellsbeer.com

The oldest surviving
microbrewery east of Colorado,
Bell's (formerly Kalamazoo
Brewing) has grown nearly
700-fold since its first sales
in 1985. Bell's has built a
new brewing facility outside
Kalamazoo, but the original
brewery remains. Bell's beers
are famous for their intensity,
although the brewery flagship
is wheat-based.

### Expedition Stout

IMPERIAL STOUT 11.5% ABV
Begins with an intense blast of dark fruit
(figs and plums) that turns into chocolate,
roasted coffee, and port.

### Oberon Ale

WHEAT BEER 5.8% ABV
A summer refresher. Zesty, with orange
rind in the aroma, and delicate spiciness
behind that. A crisp, sharp finish.

# Bere Romania

Str. Manastur Nr. 2-6, Cluj
Napoca, **ROMANIA**
www.sabmiller.com

Now a subsidiary of SABMiller,
this brewery first opened in 1878.
Its main brand, Ursus,
is advertised under the slogan
"The King of Romanian Beers".
Each September the town
of Cluj Napoca, in the heart
of Transylvania, hosts a
beer festival.

**BREWING SECRET** These beers are
fermented using Bavarian yeast.

## Ursus Premium Pils
PILSNER 5.2% ABV
Lively carbonation, a malty aroma, hints
of fresh hops and bread, and lemony
notes in the finish.

## Timisoreana
LAGER 5% ABV
A light yellow, easy-drinking beer that
doesn't challenge the senses. Made to a
recipe from 1718.

# Berg

Berg Brauerei Ulrich Zimmermann,
Brauhausstr. 2, 89548 Ehingen-Berg,
**GERMANY**
www.bergbier.de

Berg, founded in 1757, is family-
owned and one of the smallest
breweries in Germany.

**BREWING SECRET** Berg makes use
of corn in brewing, which is supplied
by an organic farm nearby.

### Berg Original
LAGER **4.8%** ABV
Its smooth, dry taste makes this beer
the most popular brand offered by
the brewery.

### Berg Märzen
MÄRZEN **6.1%** ABV
A typical strong beer. The taste is very
hearty, not least because of its high dose
of hops.

# Bergquell

Weststr. 7, Löbau, **GERMANY**
www.bergquell-loebau.de

With its long brewing tradition, the Bergquell Brauerei Löbau has played an important role in the Lausitz region since 1846. It is also one of the most advanced breweries in the whole of Germany and is well known for its wide range of special beers.

**BREWING SECRET** The special beers have an international following.

### Kirsch Porter
PORTER 4.2% ABV
A black beer with a cherry flavour and typical porter qualities. Malty and full-bodied.

### Lausitzer Porter
PORTER 4.4% ABV
Typical porter with a dry, roasted malt taste. It is full-bodied and not too heavy; dark coloured and a little bit sweet.

# Berkshire

12 Railroad Street South, Deerfield, Massachusetts 01373, **USA**
www.berkshirebrewingcompany.com

Western Massachusetts' local brewery (although its beers are increasingly easy to find in Boston). BBC handles almost all its own distribution, guaranteeing that its beer will be fresh and retain a subtle, balanced complexity that begins with open fermentation.

**BREWING SECRET** These pure, unfiltered beers must be kept refrigerated.

## Drayman's Porter
PORTER **6.2%** ABV
Coffee-like aromas, a complex middle (chocolate and toffee), and a pleasantly bitter finish.

## Raspberry Strong Ale
FRUIT BEER **9%** ABV
Brewed with fresh berries and released for Valentine's Day. Scarily nicknamed "Truth Serum".

# Berliner Kindl-Schultheiss

Indira-Ghandi-Str. 66-69, 13053
Berlin, **GERMANY**
www.berliner-kindl.de

The union of the Berliner Kindl and Berliner Schultheiss breweries in 2006 was symbolic for Germany, whose breweries had declined through post-War division. The merger has generated a great many new brands, produced in one of the most modern brewing facilities in Germany.

### Märkischer Landmann

SCHWARZBIER 4.9% ABV

Black and highly malty, but without any bitterness. A genuine original of the Märkish region.

### Bockbier

BOCK 7% ABV

Golden, strong, and not too sweet; pleasant, with a smooth finish – a typical bock.

# Bernard

5 Května č.1, 396 01 Humpolec,
**CZECH REPUBLIC**
www.bernard.cz

While reviving 16th-century Humpolec brewery in 1991, Stanislav Bernard and two partners took the daring decision to produce traditional unpasteurized beers using microfiltration. Since then, awards and an expanding export market have followed.

**BREWING SECRET** Bernard has its own floor maltings and uses spring water.

## Celebration / Sváteční Ležák
**PREMIUM LAGER 5% ABV**
Delicate herb-like hop and yeast aromas overlay a peppery bitterness for a grassy finish.

## Amber / Jantarový Ležák
**AMBER BEER 4.4% ABV**
Brewed using caramalt for a nutty bitterness, offset by toffee aromas and a honeyed palate.

# Big Sky

5417 Trumpeter Way, Missoula,
Montana 59808, **USA**
www.bigskybrew.com

Three partners successfully
combined a quality ale with a
clever name (albeit one it had
to defend in lawsuits lodged by
Canadian brewer Moosehead) and
an attractive label. Big Sky has
grown quickly into a regional
brewery selling beer from Alaska
to Minnesota, three-quarters of it
their flagship brown ale.

## Moose Drool
BROWN ALE 5.3% ABV
Dark fruits and nuts mingle with
chocolate; sweetness moderated by earthy
hop notes. Chocolate-brown with a
medium body.

## Scape Goat Pale Ale
PALE ALE 4.7% ABV
Biscuity, fruity, and spicy on the palate,
balanced by moderate bitterness. Short
but dry finish.

# Birrificio Italiano

Via Castello 51, 22070 Lurago
Marinon (CO), **ITALY**
www.birrificio.it

Agostino Arioli founded his
renowned brewpub in 1994 with
his brother Stefano and other
friends. His pils and bock soon
became cult favourites. He brews
a large range of seasonal beers
such as a sparkling blackcurrant
lager and a cask-conditioned
ale spiced with cinnamon and
ginger. The restaurant serves
great regional food and has
live music.

### Scires
**CHERRY ALE 7% ABV**
Whole black Vignola cherries, lactic
bacteria, wild yeast, and wood chips
create this fantastic sour beer.

### Fleurette
**FLAVOURED LIGHT ALE 3.7% ABV**
Made with barley, wheat, and rye,
and flavoured with rose and violet
petals, elderberry juice, black pepper,
and citrus honey.

# Bischoff

Wellerhof, 50321 Brühl,
**GERMANY**
www.bischoff-koelsch.de

This privately owned brewery
was established in farm buildings
at the beginning of the 1960s, in
an area of Brühl, near Cologne,
that has been inhabited since
Roman times.

**BREWING SECRET** The brewery's kölsch
is a speciality of the Cologne region and
is traditionally served in a tall,
narrow glass.

## Bischoff Kölsch

KÖLSCH **4.9%** ABV
Clear golden colour; fresh and sweet,
with light notes of hops.

## Radler

BEER BLEND **2.5%** ABV
Clear yellow in colour, with lemonade-
citrus aromas. It is sparkling and
very refreshing.

# Bischofshof

Heitzerstr. 2, 93049 Regensburg,
**GERMANY**
www.bischofshof.de

The Bischofshof brewery started
life attached to Regensburg
Cathedral. Records show that
it was brewing in 1230 for the
Bishop. At the beginning of
the 20th century it moved to
a new location in order to
expand. Nowadays, Bischofshof
beer is produced in one of the
most modern facilities in the
brewing industry.

### Weissbier Hell
WHEAT BEER **5.1%** ABV
An old Bavarian speciality: fresh, clear,
sparkling, and slightly sweet – in a
pleasant way.

### Bischofshof Pils
PILSNER **5.1%** ABV
Creamy foam and a light, sparkling
start. Good bitter taste; light aromas
of fine hops.

# Bitburger

Römermauer. 3, 54634 Bitburg/
Eifel, **GERMANY**
www.bitburger.de

Founded in 1817, Bitburger is
a pilsner specialist. It is well
known through international
sponsorship of sporting events,
and is widely regarded as the
best brewery for pilsner
on draught.

**BREWING SECRET** The company always
uses two-row summer barley, and its
testing brewery is unique in Germany.

### Premium Pils
**PILSNER 4.8% ABV**
A clear, typical pilsner with a light, bitter
taste; smooth, but very dry. On draught
it is fresh and elegant.

### Bitburger Light
**PILSNER 2.8% ABV**
The light sister of the premium. Though
only 2.8% ABV, it is full-bodied, with a
fresh cask taste.

# Black Sheep

Masham, North Yorkshire,
HG4 4EN **ENGLAND**
www.blacksheepbrewery.com

The Theakston family has
brewed in Masham, North
Yorkshire, for six generations,
but a loss of independence led to
Paul Theakston stepping aside.
He then established Black Sheep
in a former maltings sitting
high above the River Ure. Since
1992, Black Sheep has enjoyed
continuous growth, physically
and in reputation, resulting in a
£5m doubling of capacity in 2006.

### Black Sheep Ale
BITTER **4.4**% ABV
Full-flavoured, with a rich, fruity
aroma, bitter-sweet malty taste, and
long, dry finish.

### Riggwelter
PREMIUM BITTER **5.9**% ABV
A strong, complex, fruity bitter,
with dashes of pear drops and hints
of liquorice.

# Blaugies

435, Rue de la Frontière,
B7370 Dour-Blaugies, **BELGIUM**
www.brasseriedeblaugies.com

Hard by the French border, Blaugies is another small family brewery in which the children have taken over from the parents – who, in this case, started up the business in 1988. The aim of De Blaugies is to produce beers in the style of the region, and the brewery often creates highly unusual brews.

### La Moneuse

SAISON 8% ABV
Down-to-earth, spicy Hainaut brew: yeasty, estery; strong for a *saison*, with the characteristic metallic tang.

### Bière Darbyste

FLAVOURED ALE 5.4% ABV
Fig's juice? Alcoholic variant of Yesteryear, a non-alcoholic brew. Sweet only when fresh.

# Blonder Sörgyar

Futca 9 Vonyarcvashegy, **HUNGARY**
www.blonder.hu

One of a handful of
microbreweries to have emerged
in recent years in Hungary,
Blonder Sörgyar is situated close
to Lake Balaton, the largest
lake in central Europe. As
well as beer brewed on the
premises, this roadside inn
offers accommodation and has
a restaurant. The food is very
Hungarian – wholesome, and a
fine accompaniment to the beer.

### Világos
LAGER **5.6**% ABV
Yellow in colour, this is a strong, grainy
beer with an overt sweetness. Somewhat
rough at the edges but it works well with
Hungarian cuisine.

# J Boag & Son

39 William Street, Launceston,
Tasmania 7250, **AUSTRALIA**
www.boags.com.au

From a once-moribund regional
brewery, Boag's has ridden a
wave of popularity since the
launch of James Boag's Premium
Lager in 1994. Lagers comprise
the bulk of production, but
Boag's has rolled out some
fine limited-edition ales in recent
years. The brewery was acquired
by the Lion Nathan group in
late 2007.

### Wizard Smith's Ale
BITTER ALE 5% ABV
A solid malt backbone, with toffee and
spicy hop notes, is rounded out by a
significant bitterness.

# Bockor

Kwabrugstraat 5, B8510 Bellegem,
**BELGIUM**
www.bockor.be

This brewery is probably best
known for its Jacobins (would-be
lambics that use spontaneous
fermentation). However, the
brewery turns out a whole range
of other beers, not least a
traditional style oud bruin,
created by former head brewer
Omer Vander Ghinste. Bockor
are currently revamping the
range of beers.

### Bellegems Bruin

MIXED FERMENTATION BEER **5.5%** ABV
Oud bruin relies both on wild and
cultivated yeasts. The result: a beer in
which flavours of berries, wood, and
lactic sourness abound.

# Bøgedal Bryghus

Høllundvej 9, DK-7100 Vejle,
**DENMARK**
www.boegedal.com

This farmhouse is the world's only commercial brewery producing the old Danish style of "Goodbeer", a strong, rich beer dating back to before the industrial age. The same recipe is always followed, and yet no two beers are alike, hence they are numbered rather than named.

**BREWING SECRET** Bøgedal is Scandinavia's only all-gravity brewery.

## Brew No. 127

DARK ALE **6.3%** ABV

Smells of prunes and citrus. Fills the palate and lingers on with a faint smoky aftertaste.

## Brew No. 121

PALE ALE **5.9%** ABV

Light amber in colour with compact carbonation. Aromatic sweetness reaveals notes of honey, citrus, and fine wine.

# Boon

Fonteinstraat 65,
B1520 Lembeek, **BELGIUM**
www.boon.be

In 1975, when lambic-based beers
and lambic brewers were dying
out, Frank Boon took over the De
Vits range. Deemed crazy, he still
proves his detractors wrong, by
constantly growing and
improving his business.

**BREWING SECRET** Most Boon beers are
deemed "oude", meaning "in the old style"
of unadulterated lambics.

### Geuze Boon Mariage Parfait
GUEUZE 8% ABV
"Perfect marriage", meaning the lambics,
of course, resulting in the brewers'
favourite dry gueuze.

### Boon Oude Kriek
KRIEKEN 6.5% ABV
A fully unsweetened krieken (sour
cherry) lambic, which makes this beer
a delight for tongue and eyes.

# Boon Rawd

999 Samsen Road, Bangkok,
10300 **THAILAND**
www.boonrawd.co.th

Boon Rawd was founded in 1933
by Phraya Bhirom Bhakdi, who
had toured Germany and
Denmark to learn about brewing.
The brewery is still owned by the
Bhirom-Bhakdi family. The
company operates three
breweries in Thailand.

## Singha
LAGER 6% ABV
A full-bodied barley malt beer with
a strong hop character. Clean to taste,
it complements spicy food.

## Singha Light
LAGER 3.5% ABV
Lacks the complexity and vitality of its
stronger stablemate. It is pale yellow of
hue and thin to taste.

# Boscos

Various locations, **USA**
www.boscosbeer.com

Since 1992 this brewpub chain
has been a leader in promoting
greater knowledge of beer in
the mid-south. Its pubs feature
English-inspired cask-conditioned
ales, with customers invited to
participate as cellermen.

**BREWING SECRET** Flaming Stone's
brewing process involves red-hot chunks
of granite being plunged into the wort
to caramelize the sugars.

### Flaming Stone Beer
STEINBEER **4.8**% ABV
Brewed in the manner of German
stein beers. Caramel, toffee, and
nuts throughout. Smoky, dry finish.

### Hefeweizen
HEFEWEIZEN **4.8**% ABV
Classic bubblegum and banana nose;
softer fruity (more banana) and creamy
flavours, with underlying spices
including light clove notes.

# Bosteels

Kerkstraat 96,
B9255 Buggenhout, **BELGIUM**
www.bestbelgianspecialbeers.be

It is now the seventh generation
of the Bosteels family that owns
and runs this brewery. In recent
times, they have shown a flair for
flowing with fashion – not only
in the beers, but also with
spectacular glassware.

**BREWING SECRET** Tripel Karmeliet, one
of the flagship beers, uses three grains in
the mash: barley, wheat, and oats.

### Tripel Karmeliet
ABBEY TRIPLE 8% ABV
Smoked and spicy nose announces a
malt-dominated brew with a roasted
character – unusual for a pale beer.

### Deus Brut Des Flandres
BELGIAN STRONG ALE 11.5% ABV
The Dom Perignon lookalike bottle shows
that this is aimed at upmarket drinkers;
dry and spritzy.

# Boulder

2880 Wilderness Place, Boulder,
Colorado 80301, **USA**
www.boulderbeer.com

The first US microbrewery
outside of California, Boulder
has been something of a poster
child for the "movement" because
its partners began brewing in
a goat shed and it relied on
the largesse of domestic giant
Coors to acquire ingredients.
Boulder Beer is available in much
of the US, and emphasizes its
Colorado roots.

### Planet Porter

PORTER 5.1% ABV
The brewery's original beer. Dark fruit
aromas and flavours. Subdued roasted
malts and bitterness.

### Hazed & Infused

PALE ALE 4.85% ABV
As hazy as promised – hops in suspension
– supported by a bouquet of citrus,
flowers, and spices.

# Bourganel

7 avenue Claude Expilly,
07600 Vals les Bains, **FRANCE**
www.bieres-bourganel.com

In 1997 Christian Bourganel,
a drinks distributor in the
Ardèche, decided to develop a
range of blonde artisan beers
flavoured with regional produce.

**BREWING SECRET** Unusual ingredients
include chestnuts (*marrons*), bilberries
(*myrtilles*), nougat from Montélimar and
Verveine du Velay liqueur, which
is flavoured with verbena.

### Bourganel au Nougat
FLAVOURED LAGER 5% ABV
An amazing nougat bouquet and, in the
mouth, the flavour of grilled almonds.

### Bourganel aux Marrons
FLAVOURED LAGER 5% ABV
An amber beer; elegant, very fruity and
refreshing, with a hint of vanilla as well
as chestnut.

# Brains

Crawshay Street, Cardiff,
Glamorgan, CF10 1SP **WALES**
www.sabrain.com

A major force in regional
brewing, Brains is tremendously
proud of its Welsh heritage. Ales
are produced in a traditional
fashion at the company's
landmark Cardiff Brewery, to
which it was relocated in 2000
from the nearby Old Brewery,
where the famous "pint of
Brains" had been produced for
more than 100 years.

### Brains SA Gold
BEST BITTER 4.2% ABV
Its spirit aroma blends gentle malt
and spiced hop with malt-rich and
fruit flavours.

### Brains Bitter
BITTER 3.7% ABV
Rich amber colour, with subtle malt and
crisp hop aromas. Well balanced, with
some bitterness.

# Brakspear

Witney, Oxfordshire,
OX28 4DP **ENGLAND**
www.brakspear.co.uk

The long-established Brakspear
Brewery closed its Henley
operation in 2002, but the
production of its beers was taken
on by Wychwood Brewery.

**BREWING SECRET** Wychwood uses
Brakspear's original equipment
to brew these beers, including
the unique "double drop" wooden
fermenting vessels, and its
complex yeast strain.

### Brakspear Bitter
BITTER 3.4% ABV
An initial malt and well-hopped
bitterness develops into a bitter-sweet
and fruity finish.

### Brakspear Special
STRONG BITTER 4.3% ABV
Full-bodied, with a hint of sweetness and
dry hop bitterness before finishing
citrus-fruity.

# Brahma

Rua São Cristóvão, 1221, São Cristóvão, Rio de Janeiro, **BRAZIL**
www.brahma.com

The Portuguese brought beer to Brazil at the beginning of the 19th century but it was Swiss immigrant Joseph Villager who first brewed Brahma in 1888. Named after the Hindu god, Brahma has grown to be one of the world's most drunk beers. The company is now part of Anheuser-Busch InBev.

### Brahma
LAGER **4.8**% ABV
Low in bitterness and light to drink, it has a subtle fruity aroma and no aftertaste.

### Antarctica
LAGER **4.9**% ABV
Light in colour, bitterness, and aroma, it is an easy drinking beer.

# Braugold

Schillerstr. 7, 99096 Erfurt,
**GERMANY**
www.braugold.de

The brewery was founded in
1822, and acquired other
breweries over time – up until
1948, the point at which it was
nationalized by the GDR. After
Reunification in 1990, Braugold
was purchased by the Licher
Privatbrauerei.

**BREWING SECRET** The brewers
follow recipes from the famous
Thüringer brewery.

## Braugold Spezial
**PILSNER 4.9% ABV**
Has the typical golden colour and
dryness of a pilsner; highly aromatic
with a balanced bitterness of hops
on the palate.

## Braugold Bock
**BOCK 6.5% ABV**
Its balanced, bitter aroma and strong
flavour are typical of a bock.

# Brewer's Art

1106 N. Charles Street, Baltimore,
Maryland 21201, **USA**
www.thebrewersart.com

Housed in a grand 1902
townhouse in the Mount Vernon
area, The Brewer's Art serves
Belgian-inspired house beers
and an outstanding selection of
continental (primarily Belgian)
beers in a comfortable dining
atmosphere. It recently began
brewing and bottling some
of its beer under contract
in Pennsylvania.

### Green Peppercorn Tripel
TRIPLE 10% ABV
Effervescent and full of life. Fruity and
spicy, a bit of candy sweetness, subdued
pepper and a dryish finish.

### Resurrection
DOUBLE 7% ABV
Caramel, dark fruits on the palate, and
surprising citrus notes. The yeast in the
first batch "died" and was "resurrected",
hence the name.

# BridgePort

1313 Northwest Marshall Street,
Portland, Oregon 97209, **USA**
www.bridgeportbrew.com

BridgePort Brewing holds the trademark of Oregon's Oldest Craft Brewery, and its India Pale Ale has come to define northwestern US beer character. Despite several expansions it remains Portland-oriented. It dedicates each release of Old Knucklehead, its seasonal barley wine, to a different local personality.

### India Pale Ale

INDIA PALE ALE 5.5% ABV
Citrussy from the outset. Solid malt backbone, delicate fruits (peaches and apples). Complex hoppy finish.

### Black Strap Stout

STOUT 6% ABV
A rich blend of black strap molasses, chocolate and coffee, finishing with roasted bitterness.

# Brinkhoff

Lütgendortmunder Hellweg 242,
44388 Dortmund, **GERMANY**
www.brinkhoffs.de

From its humble origins in
1844 as a small home brewery,
Brinkhoff has had more than
160 years of success, to become
a brand known far beyond its
hometown of Dortmund, one
of the beer capitals in the world.
Brinkhoff's No. 1 is a notable
name for every lover of the
special pilsners from this region.

### Brinkhoff's No. 1

**PILSNER 5% ABV**
Typical bitter aromas of a pilsner.
Smooth, slightly sparkling, with
a golden-yellow colour.

### Brinkhoff's Radler

**BEER BLEND 2.5% ABV**
Honey-coloured, sparkling and pleasant
with citrus aromas; very refreshing and
not too sweet.

# OREGON, USA

The term "Beervana" is often used to describe Oregon's culture of craft beer. Beer touring opportunities abound, and it would be possible to spend weeks travelling and never drink the same beer twice. This three-day trail starts in the seaside town of Newport, which is home to the iconic Rogue Ales brewery. It continues the next day with scenic stops on the way to Portland, then concludes with a full day in the Rose City. For more information visit www.oregonbeer.org.

 DAY 1: **NEWPORT AND ROGUE ALES**
Rogue Ales Public House is located on OSU Drive, right in the centre of the working seaport of Newport. There are plenty of bed and breakfasts to choose from in this friendly town, including Rogue's "Bed and Beer" apartments, above the public house. The public house is also the place to book in for one of the brewery tours, which commence at 3pm daily. *2320 OSU Drive, Newport (www.rogueales.com)*

 DAY 2: **PELICAN PUB & BREWERY**
The scenic 77-km (48-mile) drive from Newport to Pacific City easily occupies a morning, so you should arrive just in time for lunch at the Pelican Pub & Brewery. The brewery-restaurant is located on the shoreline of Pacific City, where there are outstanding views of the oft-photographed Haystack Rock and Cape Kiwanda. *33180 Cape Kiwanda Drive, Pacific City (www.pelicanbrewery.com)*

DAY 2: **GOLDEN VALLEY BREWERY & PUB**
The scenic route to McMinnville passes through the Willamette Valley, one of the nation's premier wine-growing regions. The Golden Valley Brewery & Pub offers ales, sometimes aged in wine barrels. *980 East 4th St, McMinnville*

DAY 3: **PORTLAND**
With more than three dozen breweries in the metropolitan region, it is little wonder residents of Portland like to say they live in "Beervana". Here are some you could visit on Day 3 of this trail.

**Hair of the Dog**
This tiny brewery uses equipment not originally designed for brewing. Visits by appointment. *4509 SE 23rd Avenue, Portland (www.hairofthedog.com)*

**Widmer (see p366)**
Visit the brewery's Gasthaus restaurant to sample the full line-up of beers – including the Alt intended to be the brewery flagship before its Hefeweizen became an American standard. The brewery offers tours on Fridays and Saturdays. *929 North Russell, Portland*

**BridgePort (see p84)**
Oregon's oldest surviving brewery helped turn the Pearl District into a hip locale. *1313 Northwest Marshall Street, Portland*

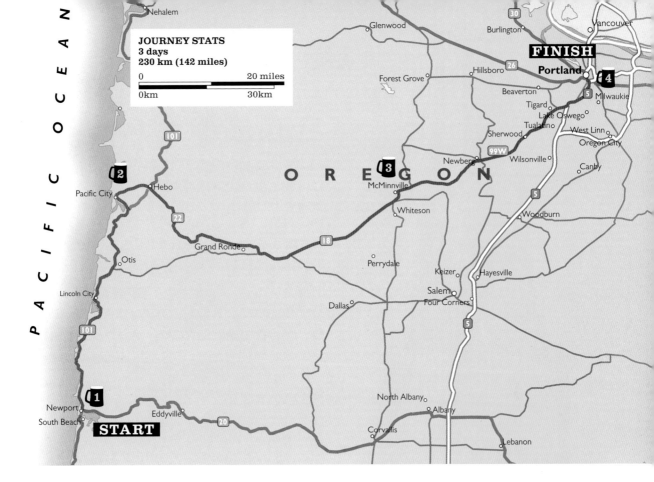

JOURNEY STATS
3 days
230 km (142 miles)

0 ____ 20 miles
0km ____ 30km

## Higgins Brewpub

Greg Higgins uses local produce for his widely praised menu, which pairs well with Oregon beers and wines. *1239 SW Broadway, Portland*

## Green Dragon Bistro and Pub

This relative newcomer quickly became an instant hit with a trendy crowd. Offers a constantly-changing selection of beers not necessarily found elsewhere, served by a knowledgeable staff. *928 SE 9th Avenue, Portland*

## Horse Brass Pub

A Portland institution since 1976, the Horse Brass is a sprawling tribute to both the English pub and Oregon beer, offering 52 selections on draught. The pub is especially popular with the late-night crowd. *4534 SE Belmont Street, Portland*

# Bristol

1647 South Tejon, Colorado Springs, Colorado 80906, **USA**
www.bristolbrewing.com

Since opening in 1994, Bristol Brewing has been the beer hub in Colorado Springs, as others have come and gone. It ventured into experimenting with barrels ahead of many US breweries.

**BREWING SECRET** It has won awards with a beer made using wild yeast and lactic acid bacteria from raspberries picked in nearby Cheyenne Canyon.

## Winter Warlock
OATMEAL STOUT **6.5%** ABV
Toasted marshmallows and chocolate up front, creamy chocolate and roasted flavours on the palate.

## Laughing Lab
SCOTTISH ALE **5.3%** ABV
Medium-bodied, with sweet notes of caramel and toffee and a lingering impression of smoke. Best on tap.

# Brøckhouse

Høgevej 6, DK-3400 Hillerød,
**DENMARK**
www.broeckhouse.dk

A fast-growing and popular microbrewery to the north of Copenhagen, established in 2002. It was the goal of owner Allan Poulsen, a former IT engineer, to create something different from ordinary Danish pilsner.

**BREWING SECRET** Poulsen uses quality ingredients and British, German, and Belgian brewing traditions to create exciting and memorable brews.

### Brøckhouse IPA
INDIAN PALE ALE 6% ABV
Top-fermented ale brewed with three varieties of hops to achieve a sweet, balanced complexity.

### Brøckhouse Esrum Kloster
ABBEY ALE 7.5% ABV
Developed with the monks of Esrum Abbey. Strong nose; sweet, spicy flavour with hints of aniseed, lavender, rosemary, and juniper.

# Brooklyn

1 Brewers Row, 79 North 11th
Street, Brooklyn,
New York 11211, **USA**
www.brooklynbrewery.com

While Brooklyn Brewery pays
homage to New York's rich
brewing history, it is very much
a 21st-century business, and
occupies New York's first
commercial building to derive all
of its electricity from wind power.
The brewery's bottled beers are
made under contract in upstate
New York, while brewmaster
Garrett Oliver regularly produces
seasonals and a reserve series at
the brewery, sold on draught
throughout the region.

### Brooklyner Weisse

HEFEWEIZEN 5.1% ABV
Effervescent and banana-fruity from the
start, backed up with spices, hops, and
gentle clove notes.

### Local 1

BELGIAN STRONG GOLDEN ALE 9% ABV
An explosion of aromas and flavours of
fruits and spices, and a complex texture, all
brought together with a chalky-dry finish.

# Brouwerij 't IJ

Funenkade 7, 1018 AL Amsterdam,
**NETHERLANDS**
www.brouwerijhetij.nl

Amsterdam's favourite micro
is now the city's oldest brewery,
even though it was founded
only in 1985. Strong Belgian-
style ales form the backbone of
the output, though there's also
a pils and a witbier. Set in an
old windmill, the taproom is
thronged on warm summer
afternoons, its outdoor
seating taken up by drinkers
enjoying the lowest beer prices
in Amsterdam.

### Turbock
**DOPPELBOCK 9% ABV**
Packed with dark fruits and molasses
sweetness, the trademark IJ spiciness
adds a dimension not found in
German bocks.

### Columbus
**STRONG ALE 9% ABV**
A balance of biscuity malt, coriander,
lemon, and resinous, minty hops.
Assertive, but not overpowering.

# BrowArmia

Ul. Królewska 1,
Warszawa, 00-065, **POLAND**
www.browarmia.pl

Opened in 2005, this fine
brewpub has a vibrant
atmosphere – busy, convivial,
and loud on music nights. Polish
food with a modern twist is a
speciality to match the beers
on tap. Six beers are currently
brewed in the smart cellar
brewery, with six more planned
for the future.

### Pszenciczne
PALE ALE **4.8%** ABV
Not quite a Burton ale, it is strongly
hopped in the kettle before being
dry-hopped in the lagering tank.

### Raspberry Wheat Beer
WHEAT BEER **5%** ABV
The house wheat beer is in the
Bavarian style, with the addition
of fresh raspberries. The fruit adds
a refreshing, zesty tartness.

# Bucher Bräu

Elsenthaler Str. 5-7,
9441 Grafenau, **GERMANY**
www.bucher-braeu.de

A medium-sized brewery that moved to the heart of the Bavarian Forest in 1982 after outgrowing its premises in the centre of Grafenau. It has been owned by the Bucher family since 1863 (now in its fifth generation).

**BREWING SECRET** The natural cloudiness of the Hefeweizen comes from the yeast added at the time of bottling.

## Grafenauer Hefeweizen
WHEAT BEER 5.2% ABV
Fresh and sparkling. The light taste of yeast is fine and aromatic. There is a little sweetness.

## Helles
LAGER 4.9% ABV
Clear yellow beer, slightly bitter, with a reasonable sweetness, and a taste of the finest hops. A rather strong but rounded finish.

# Budels

Nieuwstraat 9,
6020 AA Budel, **NETHERLANDS**
www.budels.nl

Budels is among the few established, predominantly bottom-fermenting Dutch breweries. Started in 1870, the business is currently run by the fourth generation of the founding Aerts family.

**BREWING SECRET** In recent years Budels has diversified into top-fermenting beers, such as kölsch, altbier, and an abbey-style dubbel.

## Budels Lager
PILS 5% ABV
A gentle, piney hop aroma is followed by fruity, sweetish taste; perhaps closer to a helles than a pils.

## Budels Capucijn
ABBEY-STYLE DOUBLE 6.5% ABV
Sweet toasted malt aromas are complemented by bitterness, dates, and the merest hint of smoke.

# Budweiser Budvar

Karolíny Světle 4, 370 21
České Budějovice,
**CZECH REPUBLIC**
www.original-budweiser.cz

The town of České Budějovice (Budweis) has been a home of brewing since 1265. Today, the Budějovický (Budweiser) Budvar product name has Protected Geographical Indicator status within the EU (like Cognac and Parma ham), but in the USA, where Anheuser-Busch's Budweiser is trademarked, it is called Czechvar.

### Budweiser Budvar / Czechvar
PREMIUM LAGER 5% ABV
Spritzy, with an attractive head, floral and grapefruit fruitiness on the nose, and a dry, biscuit malt palate.

### Czech Dark Lager
DARK BEER 4.7% ABV
Its distinct malty flavour develops a cinnamon spiciness before rolling into biscuit undertones.

# Caldera

540 Clover Lane, Ashland,
Oregon 97520, **USA**
www.calderabrewing.com

Although it's been around since
1997, Caldera has enjoyed
increased visibility and
distribution since 2005, when it
became the first microbrewery in
Oregon to install a small-run line
for its distinctively packaged
canned beers.

**BREWING SECRET** Caldera sets itself
apart by continuing to use whole
hop flowers in all its beers.

## IPA
INDIA PALE ALE **6.7%** ABV
Makes a large hop impression without
being heavy-handed. Citrus, pine, and
grapefruit from start to finish.

## Pilsener
PILSNER **5%** ABV
Gets eight full weeks of lagering.
Floral aroma, with just an initial hint
of sulphur, with a crisp, hoppy flavour
and finish.

# Caledonian

42 Slateford Road, Edinburgh,
EH11 1PH **SCOTLAND**
www.caledonian-brewery.co.uk

The Caledonian attitude to brewing beer is similar to that of drinking it – the longer you've been doing it, the more quality you demand. It is the sole survivor of some 40 breweries that once resided in Edinburgh.

**BREWING SECRET** Caledonian is one of the last breweries to use traditional direct-fired coppers to boil the wort.

## Caledonian 80 Shilling

SCOTTISH HEAVY **4.2%** ABV
Russett-brown and typically malt-led, with an underlay of raspberry and suggestion of chocolate.

## Deuchars IPA

INDIA PALE ALE **3.8%** ABV
A strident hop aroma, with citrus notes and a degree of maltiness that never wavers.

# Cantillon

Gheudestraat 56, B1070 Brussel/
Anderlecht, **BELGIUM**
www.cantillon.be

As early as 1900, the Cantillon
family had beer blending
facilities here, in the old
southern suburbs of Brussels.
In 1970, Jean-Pierre Van Roy, who
had married Claude Cantillon,
took over the business, becoming
a staunch defender of old-style
brewing. His son Jean, however,
has shown in the last 10 years or
so that the brewery is not averse
to experimentation, on occasion
using fresh hops, and even
American "C-hops" – both
anathema to the lambic tradition.

## Cantillon Gueuze
ORGANIC LAMBIC 5% ABV
Nose of citrus, horse blanket, wood, and
hay; woody flavours, with green fruit and
some sulphur; sour and tart in mouthfeel.

## Lou Pepe Framboise
FRUIT BEER 5.5% ABV
A mix of lambic beer with a pure sugar
solution. One of the most intense fruit
beers on earth.

# Capital

7734 Terrace Avenue, Middleton,
Wisconsin 53562, **USA**
www.capital-brewery.com

Capital Brewery is known for its
excellent German-inspired beers
– brewed in copper kettles from
a defunct German brewery –
though some are made with
a twist. Autumnal Fire, for
instance, is a cross between a
doppelbock and an Oktoberfest-
style ale.

**BREWING SECRET** The grain for
Capital's Island Wheat is grown on an
island in Lake Michigan.

## Munich Dark

DARK LAGER **5.4**% ABV
Malt-accented, with early hints of caramel
and nuts. Building richness with
chocolate-toffee notes.

## Special Pilsner

PILSNER **4.8**% ABV
Light on the palate with a note of honey.
Lovely floral hop aromas and a sturdy
hop finish.

# Captain Lawrence

99 Castleton Street, Pleasantville, New York 10570, **USA**
www.captainlawrencebrewing.com

Brewmaster-owner Scott Vaccaro represents the newest generation of American brewers, with a formal education in brewing science, then on-the-job training in the US and England. Back in his home state he founded this brewery with the support of his family. He is at the forefront in experimention with barrel ageing.

### Xtra Gold

TRIPLE **9%** ABV

Citrus notes from Northwest hops blend seamlessly with juicy orchard fruits and a bit of candy sweetness.

### Smoked Porter

PORTER **6.4%** ABV

Smoky to start, but rich dark fruits, chocolate, and liquorice quickly emerge. Luscious palate.

# Caracole

86, Côte Marie-Thérèse, B5500
Falmignoul, **BELGIUM**
www.brasserie-caracole.be

Started in around 1990, Caracole
moved after a few years from
Namur to the present location.
The brewery offers beers in
two varieties: a "normal", and
a "bio" (organic) version.
Caracole means "snail", and
production isn't rushed – but
the beers are enjoying growing
international recognition.

### Troublette Bio
WITBIER 5% ABV
A fully organic Belgian white, with no
excess coriander, but a fine citrussy and
refreshing finish.

### Nostradamus
BELGIAN DARK ALE 9.5% ABV
Caracole's strong dark ale is a mix
of roasted, fruity, malty, and higher
alcohol notes.

# Carib

Eastern Main Road,
Champs Fleurs, **TRINIDAD**
www.caribbeer.com

The sole brewery on Trinidad
since 1957, Carib has formed
business links with InBev,
Carlsberg, and Diageo – the
owner of Guinness. The company
also has breweries in Grenada,
and St Kitts, and Nevis. The
British brought commercial
brewing to Trinidad just after
World War I; the local taste
favours sweet lagers and
strong stouts.

### Carib Lager
LAGER 5.2% ABV
Pale, but full-bodied with a rich head
formation. Slightly aromatic, balanced
between sweet and bitter.

### Carib Stag
LAGER 5.9% ABV
European style lager. It is has a pale
golden straw colour with a rich head
formation. Very sweet.

# Cascade

131 Cascade Road, South Hobart,
Tasmania 7004, **AUSTRALIA**
www.cascadebrewery.com.au

Australia's oldest operating
brewery, complete with on-site
maltings, is also the most
striking, with the castellated
sandstone building nestled in
the foothills of the sometimes
snow-capped Mount Wellington.
Now part of the Foster's empire,
Cascade attracts tens of
thousands of beer lovers
annually to its visitor centre.

## Cascade Stout

MEDIUM STOUT 5.8% ABV
Coffee notes up front, with milk chocolate
on the palate, followed by a moderately
bitter finish.

## Cascade Blonde

SUMMER ALE 4.8% ABV
Clean and crisp, with a hint of citrus
hop flavour.

# Castelain

13 rue Pasteur,
62410 Bénifontaine, **FRANCE**
www.chti.com

Founded in 1926, this family brewery was passed into the hands of Yves and Annick Castelain from their parents in 1978. Under the name of Ch'ti (local patois for a northerner), they have developed a range of strong, mellow lager beers with a long, cold secondary fermentation period.

## Maltesse

PREMIUM LAGER **7.7%** ABV

Blonde, rich, and strong, with a taste of barley, and an appealing hint of bitterness in the finish.

## Ch'ti Blonde

LAGER **6.4%** ABV

Full-bodied, with just enough bitterness to be very refreshing. Mellow and tasty.

# Castle / SAB

65 Park Lane, Sandown,
Sandtona, **SOUTH AFRICA**
www.sablimited.co.za

SAB – South African Breweries
– was founded in 1895 and began
producing its Castle Lager
brand in the mining town of
Johannesburg. The company
soon became the biggest brewer
in southern Africa. In 2002, SAB
bought Miller Brewing in the
USA, and as SABMiller it has
become one of the biggest global
drinks companies.

### Castle Lager
LAGER 5% ABV
Award-winning lager made from African
Gold Barley and Southern Star hops. It is
brewed in nine countries and sold in 40.

### Castle Milk Stout
MILK STOUT 6% ABV
Dark, highly-hopped, strong stout with
a complex taste of roasted black malts,
coffee, and caramel.

# Cereuro – Cervejeira Europeia

Estrada da Portela n°8,
2795 – 643 Carnaxide, **PORTUGAL**
www.sumolis.pt

Part of soft drinks manufacturer Grupo Sumol, this brewery was set up after the revolution of 1974, when the brewing industry was nationalized. It went into private ownership in the 1990s. The company also brews Magna, an interesting German-style dark beer, and markets Grolsch in Portugal.

### Tagus
LAGER 5.4% ABV

A clear golden colour, this beer is rich and malty with caramel overtones. Its estery nose hints of its alcoholic strength and its warming finish.

# Cervesur

Av. De la Cultura 725, Cusco, **PERU**

Based in southern Peru in the Andes, the company, which is of German origin, has been brewing since 1898 and is now part of SABMiller. It is currently being merged with SABMiller's other Peruvian company Backus & Johnson. Its main brand, Cusqueña, is Peru's best-selling lager.

**BREWING SECRET** The water for brewing comes from a source high in the Andes.

### Cusqueña
LAGER 5% ABV
Pronounced "Cus-Ken-Ya", the beer is crisp and refreshing, with a lingering lemon aroma.

# Cēsu Alus

Aldaru laukums 1, Cēsis,
4101 **LATVIA**
www.cesualus.lv

Cēsu Alus was founded in 1879 and is the oldest brewery in Latvia. In 1999 it was purchased by the Estonian brewer A Le Coq. It is now one of the largest brewers in Latvia. It has a new, state-of-the-art brewhouse, and further huge investment is being planned. The town is renowned for its beer festival, knights' tournaments, and open-air theatre performances.

### Cēsu Premium

LAGER **5.2%** ABV

A pale golden colour, it has hints of sweet grass and hops on the nose.

### Cēsu Balsam Porter

PORTER **6%** ABV

Sweet chocolate taste with hints of aromatic vanilla. In Latvia, balsam is commonly used to flavour drinks.

# Chimay

8, Route Charlemagne,
B6464 Baileux, **BELGIUM**
www.chimay.com

Though the bottling is done in
Baileux, the brewery is still in the
monastery at Forges-les-Chimay.
Since 1861, monks have brewed
here, but Chimay became the
leading Trappist brewery
through Père Theodore, who
went to Leuven University to
study brewing in a contemporary
way. Chimay never stopped
growing and is vital to the
economy of the region.

### Grande Réserve / Bleue
BELGIAN STRONG ALE **9%** ABV
Roasted malts, with some quite dominant
bitterness, and dark, ripe fruit (plums,
blue grapes), and pears.

### Chimay Tripel
ABBEY ALE **8%** ABV
Sweet, grapey taste, with bittering hops
and herbal qualities; not entirely unlike
a dry white wine.

# La Choulette

18 rue des Écoles,
59111 Hordain, **FRANCE**
www.lachoulette.com

Founded in 1885, this farmhouse brewery is a rare survivor from the thousands of breweries that existed in the region in the late 19th century. Alain Dhaussy, the current brewer, has succeeded in creating artisan beers of real quality, faithful to the traditions of northern France, but with a real sense of innovation too.

## Choulette Framboise

FRUIT BEER **6**% ABV
Refreshing, with a slight sourness. The note of ripe raspberries is present, but not too intrusive.

## Porte Du Hainaut Ambrée

AMBER ALE **7**% ABV
Medium-bodied fruity beer, with flavours of cooked apples, pears, and caramel; slight bitterness.

# Coopers

461 South Road, Regency Park,
Adelaide, South Australia 5010,
**AUSTRALIA**
www.coopersbrewery.com.au

While most Australian breweries
were progressively "lagerized"
during the 20th century, this
family-run Adelaide brewing
dynasty kept knocking out
cloudy, bottle-conditioned ales
and stouts. Since opening a new
expanded brewery in 2001,
surging demand for their beers
has driven them to become
the country's third-largest
beer maker.

### Coopers Sparkling Ale
AUSTRALIAN PALE ALE 5.8% ABV
Cloudy; fruity aromatics with a hint
of peaches; rounded, dry, yeasty finish.

### Coopers Extra Stout
DRY STOUT 6.4% ABV
Espresso and bitter chocolate notes, with
banana hints too; robustly bitter finish.

# Coors

311 10th Street, Golden,
Colorado 80401, **USA**
www.coors.com

Although it merged with Molson,
and that company now partners
SABMiller in the US, Coors has
continued to develop less
mainstream beers. Its Blue Moon
line competes with the largest
craft brands, and its SandLot
Brewery, within the Coors Field
baseball stadium in Denver,
regularly offers outstanding
traditional lagers.

### Blue Moon Belgian White

WITBIER 5.4% ABV

Citrussy sweet nose, spicy with notes of
celery. Some wheat sourness, finishing
on the sweet side.

### Barmen Pilsner

PILSNER 5% ABV

Beautiful billowing head when poured
correctly. Rich with Saaz hops, floral, and
spicy. Pleasantly grainy, with a long,
bitter finish.

# Cornelyshaff

Maison 37,9753 Heinerscheid,
**LUXEMBOURG**
www.cornelyshaff.lu

Situated in a nature park,
Cornelyshaff comprises a popular
bar, restaurant, and hotel, as well
as a brewery that is open to
visitors. It is modern, gleaming,
and energy efficient – the
cooperative that owns it prides
itself on minimizing its
environmental impact. The bar
and restaurant showcase the
beers and much farm produce
from the area.

### Ourdaller Waïssen Tarwebier
**WITBIER 4.6% ABV**
An unfiltered, cloudy wheat beer;
assertive in character, it is full of spice.

### Kornelysbéier
**RYE BEER 4.2% ABV**
A spicy aroma gives way to a strong,
deep, earthy taste brought on by the
use of rye grain.

# Crailsheimer Engelbräu

Haller Str. 29, 74564 Crailsheim,
**GERMANY**
www.engelbier.de

When this brewery was founded
by Georg Fach in 1738,
Crailsheim had 4,000 inhabitants
and 13 breweries. Fach was not
to know that his company would
become one of the most
successful in the country.

**BREWING SECRET** A survey of what
women like in a beer led to the creation
of the First Lady brand.

### First Lady
DUNKLER BOCK **5.9**% ABV
Mild, lightly bitter, and with
a harmonious malty aroma.

### Kellerbier Dunkel
DUNKEL **5.3**% ABV
Beautiful mahogany colour; aromas of
malt and yeast; full-bodied, with a taste
that is both sweet and pleasantly bitter.

# Creemore Springs

139 Mill Street, Creemore,
Ontario, L0M 1G0, **CANADA**
www.creemoresprings.com

Ownership by Molsons since
2005 has done little to lessen the
independence of this 100-year-old
brewery. The town of Creemore
nestles between the curiously
named Mad and Noisy rivers.
Every August the brewery
is a sponsor of a town-centre
party called the Copper Kettle
Festival. Regular brewery tours
are run.

### Premium Lager
LAGER 5% ABV
Soft malt and fruit flavours give way to
nutty overtones and a dry hoppy finish.

### Urbock
BOCK 6% ABV
Dark brown, with a sweet, nutty texture;
fruit aromas can be found as the beer
warms in the glass.

# Darmstädter

Goebelstr. 7, 64293 Darmstadt,
**GERMANY**
www.darmstaedter.de

The brewery stands next to the train station in Darmstadt – hence the train logo, used since 1847, and the animated steam engine on its website.

**BREWING SECRET** A revolution in the company's history was the complete change-over of all bottles to clip-tops in the year 2000.

## Darmstädter Pilsner

PILSNER **4.8%** ABV

A clear and elegant beer. A large amount of fine hops make this a typical pilsner: fresh and dry with a good bitter aroma.

## Darmstädter 1847 Zwickelbier

LAGER **4.8%** ABV

Unfiltered and cloudy with subtle aromas of fine malt and a smooth, yeasty taste.

# Darwin

Sunderland, Tyne & Wear,
SR1 2QE **ENGLAND**
www.darwinbrewery.com

The Darwin set-up is unique in that its commercial operation is complemented by a test brew plant based at the University of Sunderland. There, students on the Brewlab brewing sciences course are able to trial some 40 new beers each year. The best of them are then produced at the award-winning site.

### Darwin's Evolution

BITTER 4% ABV

Light, clean, and satisfying, with a dry, hoppy character and layers of malt throughout.

### Ghost Ale

BITTER 4.1% ABV

Golden and richly hopped, with citrus aromas dominating, followed by a well-balanced fruit piquancy.

# Deschutes

901 Southwest Simpson Avenue,
Bend, Oregon 97702, **USA**
www.deschutesbrewery.com

What began with a brewpub in 1988 quickly expanded with a separate production facility that's grown into one of the nation's largest craft breweries. As well as selling a full line of beers with notable hop character throughout the western US, Deschutes still operates its original brewpub in downtown Bend and another in Portland. A Bond Street Series of special beer releases, developed "at the pub", has further widened the brewery's portfolio.

### Mirror Pond

PALE ALE **5.2%** ABV
Grapefruit and fresh flowers at the outset. Light, clean biscuit on the palate, with generous hop flavour.

### Inversion IPA

INDIA PALE ALE **6.8%** ABV
A swirl of hop aromas (particularly orange zest). Solid, biscuity malt holds its own against bracing bitterness.

# Desnoes and Geddes

214 Spanish Town, Kingston,
**JAMAICA**
www.jamaicadrinks.com

Now owned by global drinks
giant Diageo, Desnoes and
Geddes was established by two
friends, Eugene Desnoes and
Thomas Geddes, who set up a soft
drink plant in 1918 and began
brewing in 1927 with Red Stripe.

**BREWING SECRET** Red Stripe was
originally produced as an English ale.
It didn't become popular until it was
offered as a chilled lager instead.

### Dragon Stout
SWEET STOUT 7.5% ABV
Having been primed with sugar on
bottling, the flavour is malty, with
a distinct note of molasses.

### Red Stripe
LAGER 4.7% ABV
Yellow in colour, it has a grainy aroma,
a crisp clean taste, and is best drunk
very cold.

# Dětenice

Pivovar Dětenice, 507 24 Dětenice,
**CZECH REPUBLIC**
www.krcmadetenice.cz

The castle-based brewery – once
owned by the Prague chapter
of the Knights of Malta – closed
in 1955 after several years of
nationalization, and reopened
only in 2000.

**BREWING SECRET** Beers are brewed
in direct-fired vessels and are filtered
through straw, fermented in wooden vats,
then lagered in oak barrels.

### Svetlé Detenické Pivo 12°
**PREMIUM LAGER 4% ABV**
Aromatically floral, finely structured
body; sweet malt and honey influences,
and hoppy afterglow.

### Tmavé Detenicke Pivo 13°
**DARK BEER 4% ABV**
A typically full-bodied dark lager; malty,
some spice, and faintly bitter towards
the finish.

# Diebels

Brauerei-Diebels-Str. 1,
47661 Issum, **GERMANY**
www.diebels.de

Diebels was privately owned
from 1878 until 2001, when the
brewery was taken over by global
drinks giant InBev. The
Düsseldorfer Alt is the brewery's
most famous brand and is sold
all over Germany. Other, newer
brands include a pilsner and a
cola-blended beer called Dimix.

### Diebels Alt

ALTBIER 4.9% ABV
Roasted malt aromas harmonize with a
sweet caramel taste; the finish is slightly
bitter from hops.

### Diebels Pils

PILSNER 4.9% ABV
The full-body, light bitterness, and malt
aromas are typical of a pilsner, as is the
dark golden colour.

# Dinkelacker-Schwabenbräu

Tübinger Str. 46, 70178 Stuttgart,
**GERMANY**
www.ds-kg.de

Carl Dinkelacker was the first to brew pilsner in Stuttgart at the end of the 19th century, and his contemporary Robert Leicht was the first to deliver beer by motorcar. Today, their breweries are in partnership and together form the biggest player in Baden-Württemberg.

### Dinkelacker Privat
LAGER **5.1**% ABV
A fine, smooth, and clear golden lager with a mild aroma of hops and a light note of malt.

### Dinkelacker CD-Pils
PILSNER **4.9**% ABV
Noble dry pilsner with strong aromas of hops and light malts; very harmonious and pleasant.

# Distelhäuser

Grünsfelder Str. 3, 97941
Tauberbischofsheim, **GERMANY**
www.distelhaeuser.de

The Bauer family has owned this
brewery since 1876. It is situated
on the famous "Romantic Street"
in Tauberbischofsheim, which
is closely associated with the
German Romantic period. The
long-standing success of the
brewery is due to its attention
to quality over the course of
its history.

### Distelhäuser Landbier

EXPORT **5.1**% ABV

Malty aroma and a slightly caramel taste;
it has a mild sweetness and is rounded at
the finish. Sometimes described as a
"ladies' beer".

### Distelhäuser Pils

PILSNER **4.9**% ABV

Topped by a snow-white foam, this beer
has a harmonious bitterness and a great
aroma of hops.

# Dithmarscher

Oesterstr. 18, 25709 Marne Holstein,
**GERMANY**
www.dithmarscher.de

This brewery, on the east coast of Schleswig-Holstein, has been operating for more than 230 years. It started as a small home brewery; today it is bigger, but the beers are still handmade.

**BREWING SECRET** The sparkle comes from using the charmant method of pressurized fermentation, and the addition of dry, fresh carbonic acid.

## Dithmarscher Dunkel
DUNKEL 4.9% ABV
This beer has a full-bodied charmant character and a spicy taste with notes of roastiness. A typical colour: dark mahogany.

## Dithmarscher Pils
PILSNER 4.8% ABV
A mild and spicy beer, golden-yellow in colour, slightly sparkling.

# Dixie

2401 Tulane Avenue, New Orleans,
Louisiana 70119, **USA**
www.distinguished-brands.com/
dixie.php

The 100-year-old Dixie Brewery
was the last survivor of New
Orleans' once-flourishing
brewing tradition, with some of
its beers aged in historic cypress
barrels. That is, until Hurricane
Katrina (and the subsequent
looters) devastated it in 2005. It's
not clear when it might reopen.
Meanwhile its beers are being
made at the Minhaus Craft
Brewery in Wisconsin.

## Blackened Voodoo

**SCHWARZBIER 5% ABV**
In 1991, this dark lager was briefly
banned in Texas because of the voodoo
references on its label. Smooth and
light-bodied for southern drinking, with
chocolate and toffee notes throughout.

# Döbler

Kornmarkt 6, 91438 Bad Windsheim, **GERMANY**
www.brauhaus-doebler.de

Döbler celebrated its 140th anniversary in 2007. Production was traditional until 1950, after which the brewery switched to creating young-styled beers using technologically advanced equipment.

**BREWING SECRET** The barley has come from sustainable sources since 1986.

### Land Märzen
MÄRZEN 5.4% ABV

A very light märzen; dark yellow, with a pleasant taste, not too sweet, but full-bodied with a nice yeast finish.

### Reichsstadtbier
KELLERBIER 5% ABV

Full-bodied, unfiltered, and cloudy, with a taste of yeast. It is available on draught.

# Dogfish Head

6 Cannery Village Center, Milton,
Delaware 19968, **USA**
www.dogfish.com

Dogfish Head has found a
national audience for its "extreme
beers". These have included ales
developed using research from
archaeologists; recipes featuring
unusual ingredients, from
chicory to chillies; and beers that
simply have more of everything.
The brewery recently installed
the largest wooden brewing
vessels built in America since
before Prohibition. Dogfish still
operates a brewpub in Rehoboth
Beach, where founder Sam
Calagione started in 1995.

## Midas Touch

**HISTORIC BEER 9% ABV**
The ingredients – white Muscat grapes,
honey, and saffron – create layers of
flavour, melded with subtle acidity.

## 60 Minute IPA

**INDIA PALE ALE 6% ABV**
Flagship session beer brewed with
Warrior, Amarillo, and "Mystery Hop X",
and brimming with citrus flavours.

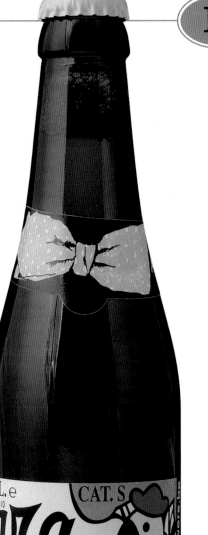

# De Dolle Brouwers

Roeselarestraat 12B,
B8600 Esen, **BELGIUM**
www.dedollebrouwers.be

By buying and renewing the old Costenoble Brewery in 1980, Kris Herteleer and his two brothers started, unknowingly, Belgium's the country's microbrewery revolution. Fame soon reached international quarters – but then the "mad brewers" never searched for simplicity, a quiet life, or easy money. "Quality does the trick" is the motto of Kris – the only remaining brewer of the original three.

## Arabier

**BELGIAN DARK ALE 9% ABV**
Fruitiness throughout, from nose to finish. Very vinous character, grapey, and clearly strong in alcohol.

## Oerbier

**SEASONAL CHRISTMAS ALE 12% ABV**
Overripe grapes, raisins, and other dried fruits. Some hoppy bitterness hiding behind lots of sweet malts; acidic lining for a great balance.

# Double Maxim

Hughton-le-Spring,
Sunderland, **ENGLAND**
www.dmbc.org.uk

After several years contracting
out the company's eponymous
beer, a new brewery was opened
in 2007 to cope with demand.
Bottling facilities are planned
for the near future.

**BREWING SECRET** Double Maxim uses
an original Vaux Brewery recipe, which
head brewer Jim Murray used when he
worked at Vaux in 1968.

### Double Maxim
BROWN ALE **4.7% ABV**
Caramel in the aroma; continues through
bittersweet flavours, then expands into
toffee notes.

### Samson
BEST BITTER **4.6% ABV**
A dependable northeast English
bitter, with a whiff of hop and a
malt-infused body.

# Dreher

Magladi ut 17, Budapest, **HUNGARY**
www.dreher.hu

For many years this brewery was run by Anton Dreher, one of the great beer innovators. In the mid-19th century, he developed the technology to ferment beer at low temperatures and created a new kind of malty amber beer, called Vienna lager. For his achievements, Dreher was dubbed "The King of Beer". The company is now owned by SABMiller.

### Dreher Classic

PILSNER 5.5% ABV

With a crisp, fresh aroma, this is a bitter, golden-yellow beer with an aroma of hops and a hint of malt.

### Dreher Bak

DUNKLER BOCK 7.3% ABV

A rich, full-bodied dark beer, notes of caramel and malt, reminiscent of bittersweet chocolate.

# Dubuisson

28, Chaussée de Mons,
B7904 Pipaix-Leuze, **BELGIUM**
www.br-dubuisson.com

Leuze is a town with three
breweries, two of them in the
Pipaix village. Dubuisson is
probably the most dynamic,
and its location, next to a major
road, has made their brewery
tap a very successful venture.
The brewery excels in high
alcohol ales, so extreme caution
is advised when drinking
these beers.

### Bush Prestige

BELGIAN STRONG ALE **13%** ABV
This oak-aged version of the Ambrée
is a true marvel in balance, despite its
impressive strength.

### Bush Ambrée

BELGIAN STRONG ALE **12%** ABV
In some markets known as "Scaldis",
this is a treacherously drinkable
alcohol-bomb.

# Ducato

Via Strepponi 50/A, 43010 Roncole Verdi di Busseto (PR), **ITALY** www.birrificiodelducato.it

Young brewer Giovanni Campari set up his microbrewery in 2007 near Giuseppe Verdi's birthplace, not far from Parma. He proved his skills from the outset, brewing four beers full of character. Further new lines are confirming Ducato as one of the most promising Italian craft breweries.

### New Morning
SAISON 5.6% ABV
Amazing *saison*, flavoured with camomile flowers. Easy-drinking and thirst-quenching, with lovely earthy notes.

### AFO
AMERICAN PALE ALE 5.2% ABV
AFO means "Ale For the Obsessed" and is dedicated to hop lovers. Nice citrus fruit aromas, caramel notes.

# Duck-Rabbit

4519 W Pine Street, Farmville, North Carolina 27828, **USA**
www.duckrabbitbrewery.com

Known for darkly intense beers, this is one of several small breweries that have thrived since North Carolina changed its law to allow beer stronger than 6% ABV. Duck-Rabbit's distinctive logo is based on an illustration by philosopher Ludwig Wittgenstein.

**BREWING SECRET** These quirky brewers say "we sing softly to the yeast".

## Baltic Porter
BALTIC PORTER 9% ABV
Caramel, toffee, blackcurrants and other dark fruits, perfectly blended. Smooth, with restrained bitterness.

## Milk Stout
STOUT 5.7% ABV
A well-integrated combination of roasted coffee beans and chocolate, held together by a creamy palate. Sweet, but not too sweet.

# Dugges Ale & Porterbryggeri

Möbelgatan 3, SE-43133 Mölndal,
**SWEDEN**
www.dugges.se

The brewery was founded in 2005 by Mikael Dugge Engström. His series of beers include Gothenburg, marrying old Swedish traditions with British and American inspiration, and Express Yourself, a collection of speciality brews with names like Holy Cow (an IPA) and Fuggedaboudit! (a brown ale).

### Dugges Avenyn Ale

AMERICAN PALE ALE 5% ABV
Aromas of hops, flowers, and citrus fruits; flavours of grapes, pine, and a hint of caramel.

### High Five!

INDIAN PALE ALE 7.5% ABV
Dark amber. Intense hop aroma; notes of strawberry jam, pine, and chocolate, and a dry bitterness.

# Dupont

Brasserie Dupont, 5 Rue Basse,
B7904 Tourpes-Leuze, **BELGIUM**
www.brasserie-dupont.com

Western-Hainaut enjoys rich soil,
and farmsteads here were huge
– usually operating a brewery
in the winter, making beer to be
consumed on the land in summer
(hence the style of beer known
as *saison*). Brasserie Dupont
became solely a brewery,
but owner Olivier Dedeycker
has re-engaged with the history
of the land, by reintroducing
farming and cheese making
into this marvellous brewery.

### Avec Les Bons Vœux

**SEASONAL WINTER ALE 9.5% ABV**
Barnyard and earthy aromas mingle with
citrus zest. Grainy flavour: fresh white
bread with nuts, spices, and walnut oil.

### Saison Dupont

**SAISON 6.5% ABV**
Formerly brewed in winter with the hot
summer months in mind – hence a dry,
refreshingly light brew.

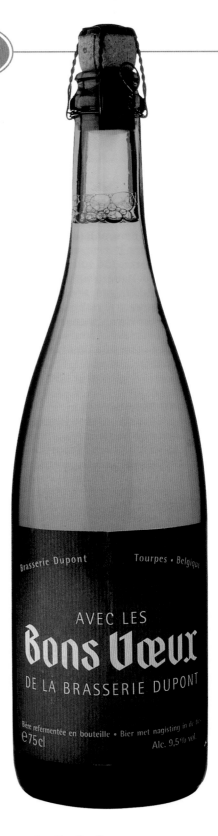

# Duvel Moortgat

Breendonkdorp 58-66, B2870
Breendonk-Puurs, **BELGIUM**
www.duvel.be

Started as a small family
brewery, Moortgat continued
producing top-fermented ale at
a time when everywhere lager
reigned. The Moortgat ale
evolved into the iconoclastic
Duvel, a beer that has become
so popular that the brewery
group renamed itself. Moortgat
now owns breweries in Belgium
and abroad.

### Duvel

BELGIAN STRONG ALE **8.5% ABV**
Sometimes dubbed "red", to distinguish
it from the filtered version, this ultra dry
ale hides its potency as no other.

### Maredsous 8°

BROWN ABBEY ALE **8% ABV**
Arguably the best from the Maredsous
Abbey range. Estery, fruity notes, and
tobacco leaf.

# Duyck

113 route Nationale, 59144 Jenlain,
**FRANCE**
www.duyck.com

Originally a farmhouse brewery, Duyck was established in 1922, producing beers in the northern *bière de garde* style – brewed and bottled in the winter for laying down and drinking in the summer. In the 1950s, the family began bottling their beers in recycled champagne bottles. Raymond Duyck, the present manager, is the fourth generation of this family of brewers.

### Jenlain Ambrée

AMBER ALE **7.5%** ABV

Full bodied, with a hint of bitterness, the mellowness of roasted malt and aromas of stewed prunes and caramel. A perfect accompaniment to food, but also an ingredient in rustic local dishes such as *Carbonnade Flamande* (beef cooked in beer).

# Echigo

3970 Fukui, Nishiura-ku, Niigata City, Niigata 953-0076, **JAPAN**
www.echigo-beer.jp

The brewers of the venerable Tsurukame saké of Niigata opened Japan's first microbrewery in February of 1995 to great fanfare. Operations have expanded from the original brewpub to a large-scale brewery with canning line today. While the canned products are well regarded, the more expensive small-production bottled products are even more highly prized.

### Echigo Pilsener
**PILSNER 5% ABV**
This reasonably priced craft beer has a rich malty flavour, moderate bitterness, and a clean, quick finish.

### Echigo Stout
**STOUT 7% ABV (PREVIOUSLY 5%)**
Higher gravity and more care in the brewing of this beer results in a brilliant interplay of rich, roasty flavours.

# Eel River

1777 Alamar Way, Fortuna,
California 95540, **USA**
www.eelriverbrewing.com

Eel River had been around less
than five years when, in 2000, it
became the first certified organic
brewery in the USA. The brewpub
added a production brewery in
nearby Scotia in 2007, moving
into an abandoned mill. The new
brewery is 100 per cent powered
by biomass – that is, mill waste
such as wood chippings, and
spent grain from brewing.

### Organic Porter
PORTER 6.3% ABV
Malty and creamy with chocolate aromas
and flavours, and lesser notes of roast
coffee beans. Robust.

### Triple Exultation
OLD ALE 9.7% ABV
Not organic. A complex nose of rich
caramel-toffee and fruit, then piney hops
assert themselves.

# Eggenberg

Eggenberg 1, A-4655 Vorchdorf,
**AUSTRIA**
www.schloss-eggenberg.at

Schloss Eggenberg is a small
castle in Upper Austria that has
been brewing for more than 500
years. A broad range of lagers
(including a non-alcoholic one)
are produced for the local
market, and some fine bock beers
are brewed for export; these
include an urbock and even a
blond version of the traditionally
dark Samichlaus beer.

### Samichlaus
DOPPELBOCK 14% ABV
Intense malt aroma, with noticeable
alcohol. Sweet and fruity (dried
cherries, figs, and plums); very little
hop character present.

### Hopfenkönig
PILSNER 5.1% ABV
Very pale, with a firm head and hay-like
spicy hop aromas. Light body followed by
some dry bitterness.

# Eggenberg

Latrán 27, 38115, Český Krumlov,
**CZECH REPUBLIC**
www.eggenberg.cz

Nowhere but in Bohemia could two towns merge over brewing disputes. Years of arguing about wheat beer privileges were resolved simply by uniting neighbours Latrán and Krumlov, and establishing a single brewery. Over time, the brewery passed from the Eggenberg family to the Schwarzenbergs and down the centuries to its present owners, Dionex.

### Eggenberg Světlý Ležák
**PREMIUM LAGER 5% ABV**
Powerfully floral with sweet butterscotch notes; zesty, firm, and delightfully balanced to a bitter finish.

### Eggenberg Tmavý Ležák
**DARK BEER 4.2% ABV**
Deep and dark, with a hop pungency, then a malty caramel and toffee bittersweet palate.

# Einbecker

Papenstr. 4, 37574 Einbeck,
**GERMANY**
www.einbecker.com

The story goes that, in 1521, Martin Luther said that Einbecker's beer was his favourite. In 1612, Bavarian dukes engaged a master brewer from Einbeck, whose beer eventually became known as bock, in a corruption of the name Einbeck.

### Ur-Bock Hell

BOCK **6.5%** ABV
The pale malt and fine hops give this classic bock a hearty taste.

### Einbecker Spezial

EXPORT **5.2%** ABV
Has the typical golden-yellow colour of an export beer. Has a fine, slightly sweet flavour.

# Emerson's Brewery

14 Wickliffe Street, Dunedin,
**NEW ZEALAND**
www.emersons.co.nz

New Zealand's most awarded micro offers an enviable portfolio of year-round beers, as well as seasonal specialities such as Taieri George, a spiced dark ale, and a US pale ale featuring American hops.

**BREWING SECRET** Emerson's delightful session beer called Bookbinder Bitter is available only on tap.

### Emerson's Old 95
BARLEY WINE 7% ABV
Robust bottle conditioned ale, with rich, toffee-like malt and resiny hops. Will reward careful cellaring.

### Emerson's Organic Pilsner
NEW WORLD PILSNER 4.9% ABV
Bursting with passion fruit and citrus. A showcase for New Zealand's Riwaka hop variety.

# Erdinger

Lange Zeile 1+3, 85435 Erding,
**GERMANY**
www.erdinger.de

This is the biggest and most famous specialist wheat beer brewery in the world. The first mention of a brewery at Erding was in 1886, but it was not until 1949 that the name Erdinger Weissbräu was used.

**BREWING SECRET** Fresh spring water and hops from the Hallertau region are used in brewing.

### Erdinger Pikantus
**DARK WEIZENBOCK 7.3% ABV**
Normally a wheat bock is sweet, but not so Erdinger's. Watch out for the ABV on this one.

### Erdinger Schneeweisse
**WINTER BEER 5.6% ABV**
Darker and heavier bodied than the normal weizen. It is available between October and February.

# Everards

Castle Acres, Narborough,
Leicestershire, LE19 1BY **ENGLAND**
www.everards.co.uk

After brewing his first pint in
1849, William Everard stated
his intention, and one that the
fifth-generation family is proud
to uphold: "No effort shall be
found wanting in the production
and supply of genuine ale of
first-rate quality". Integrity
remains king today.

**BREWING SECRET** Fuggles and
Goldings are the key hops here.

### Tiger
BITTER 4.2% ABV
Some spicy hop and caramel on the nose.
Classically bittersweet palate, with a
rounded toffeeness.

### Original
STRONG BITTER 5.2% ABV
Copper-hued, full-bodied, and a toasted
caramel aroma beckoning port wine and
fruit flavours.

# Exmoor

Wiveliscombe, Somerset,
TA4 2NY **ENGLAND**
www.exmoorales.co.uk

Exmoor was among the first
wave of microbreweries in the
early 1980s. Its fundamentals
have never altered from a
reliance on skills, investment
in innovation, and adherence
to the principles of small-batch
brewing. Being Somerset's
largest brewery positions it
as a regional producer, and
the potential of its backbone
brands is still to be fully
capitalized upon.

### Exmoor Gold

BITTER 4.5% ABV
Powerful earthy hop, lemon, and juicy
malt aromas; fruity, butterscotch
sweetness, and memorable finish.

### Exmoor Ale

BITTER 3.8% ABV
Medium-bodied, with some malt and hop
in the aroma and bitter hop aftertaste.

# Fantôme

8, Rue Préal, B5454 Soy-Erezée,
**BELGIUM**
www.fantome.be

Dany Prignon started this micro
in a shed in the Ardennes,
and while today he exports his
beers to many countries, the
shed is still the brewery's home
– though it now contains far
more equipment.

**BREWING SECRET** More works of art
than products of brewing science, many
of the beers are never brewed the same
way twice.

## Fantôme
SAISON 8% ABV
The brewery's staple blond beer: fruity,
lactic, variable, and in the style of
a *saison*.

## Black Ghost
BELGIAN STRONG DARK ALE 8% ABV
One of the few regularly seen: malty, with
fruity depths, but also flavours of cypress
and pine.

# Fässla

Obere Königstr. 19-21, 96052
Bamberg, **GERMANY**
www.faessla.de

In 1649, just a year after the end
of the Thirty Years' War, master
brewer Hans Lauer founded this
brewery in Bamberg. In modern
times, 1986 was a turning point,
when the Kalb family took over
control. Fässla's speciality beers
are well known in the region.

**BREWING SECRET** Bambergator is the
strongest beer brewed in Bamberg.

## Lagerbier
LAGER 5.5% ABV
Strong yellow in colour; fine, compact
foam; sparkling. Full-bodied and slightly
malty with a light bitter taste.

## Bambergator
DOPPELBOCK 8.5% ABV
A dark brown, full-bodied, and very
strong doppelbock, bursting with
harmonious hop bitters.

# Faust

Hauptstr. 219, 63897 Miltenberg,
**GERMANY**
www.faust.de

A typical regional family-run company. The brewery is about 350 years old and changed hands many times in the first 200 years of its history. The Fausts took over in 1895, and still own it today. There are many different styles of beer produced, some of which have won prizes.

## Schwarzviertler

**DUNKEL 5.2% ABV**

Dark, roasty, and slightly smoky. There is also caramel and a little bitter-chocolate on the tongue. It is full-bodied and has a dry finish.

## Faust Kräusen

**KELLERBIER 5.5% ABV**

A mild, full-bodied beer with a light note of honey; it is very fresh.

# Felinfoel

Llanelli, Carmarthenshire,
SA14 8LB **WALES**
www.felinfoel-brewery.com

Sitting astride the River Liedi
and leaning heavily on the
industrial traditions of south
Wales – and its workers' thirsts
– Felinfoel Brewery has been in
existence since 1878. It is famed
for producing Britain's first
canned beer in 1935. Extensive
modernization came in the
1970s, but Felinfoel is still family-
owned.

### Double Dragon
BITTER **4.2%** ABV
Invitingly rich in colour, malty and
subtly hopped, with an evenly balanced,
full-drinking nature.

### Cambrian Bitter
BITTER **3.9%** ABV
Labelled "a good honest Welsh bitter", the
bitter is full-flavoured, with balanced malt
and hop aromas.

# Fiege

Moritz Fiege, Scharnhorststr. 21-25,
44787 Bochum, **GERMANY**
www.moritzfiege.de

"We are a classic regional
brewery" says Hugo Fiege, the
boss of the company. He sees his
brewery as an ambassador for
the Ruhr region. It is an
institution offering typical local
beers – inhabitants of the Ruhr
love their beer. There is little
chance of a big global player
acquiring Fiege.

### Moritz Fiege Pils

PILSNER **4.9**% ABV
A classic pilsner with bitter aromas of
good hops, a light malty taste, and a fine
dry structure.

### Schwarzbier

SCHWARZBIER **4.9**% ABV
Elegant and with a malty sweetness,
this coffee-coloured beer has light bitter
aromas of fine hops.

# Finlandia

Suokulmantie 237, Matku,
Forsaa FI-31110, **FINLAND**
www.finlandiasahti.fi

Finlandia is a specialist brewer
of sahti, a traditional Finnish
home-brew made with rye and
other grains, flavoured with
juniper twigs and berries. Beer
enthusiasts can sample Finlandia
Sahti in Helsinki at St Urho's Pub
and the Restaurant Savotta.
The best time to do so is during
Helsinki's Sahti Week, which
takes place in May each year.

### Sahti Strong
SAHTI 10% ABV
Sweet and somewhat oily on the
palate; the juniper nose gives way
to a bubblegum aftertaste.

### Tavallinen
SAHTI 8% ABV
A deep chestnut colour, with a heavy
juniper nose and a hint of blackcurrant.

# Flensburger

Munketoft 12, 24937 Flensburg,
**GERMANY**
www.flensburger.de

Five citizens of Flensburg
founded this brewery in 1888.
During the 1970s, the brewery's
reputation was enhanced when
a comedian kept referring to a
"Flasch Flens" in his act. The
term came to be used for a bottle
of Flensburger, which at the time
was the only German beer to use
clip-top bottles.

### Flensburger Pils
PILSNER **4.8**% ABV
A typical golden pilsner – malty,
refreshing, and with slightly bitter
aromas of hops in the finish.

### Kellerbier
KELLERBIER **4.8**% ABV
Amber and cloudy, like all kellerbiers, the
Flensburger version is full-bodied and
tastes naturally fresh, slightly sweet, and
has a dry finish.

# Flossmoor Station

1035 Sterling Avenue, Flossmoor, Illinois 60422, **USA**
www.flossmoorstation.com

Brewers Matt Van Wyk and Andrew Mason have expanded on what barrel-ageing pioneer Todd Ashman started at Flossmoor Station Brewing. They offer a wide range of award-winning beers in a pub housed in a former railway station. The brewery recently launched a small range of bottled beers.

### Pullman Brown Ale
BROWN ALE 7% ABV
Brewed with hand-toasted malts and molasses. A full-bodied blend of chocolate, toffee, and dark fruit.

### De Wilde Zuidentrein
SOUR ALE 7% ABV
A Flanders brown ale, aged in an oak wine barrel on fresh raspberries for a year, dosed with wild yeasts.

# Flying Dog

2401 Blake Street, Denver,
Colorado 80205, **USA**
www.flyingdogales.com

With labels by British illustrator
Ralph Steadman, and the "gonzo"
spirit of the late Hunter S.
Thompson (both friends of
founder George Stranahan),
Flying Dog is not your average
brewery. The original brewpub
was founded in Aspen but is now
headquartered in Denver, while
the company moved brewing
operations to Frederick in
Maryland in 2008.

### Gonzo Imperial Porter
PORTER 9% ABV
Rummy, chocolatey, and almost sweet
before dry cocoa flavours and solid hop
bitterness kick in.

### Doggie Style Pale Ale
PALE ALE 5.3% ABV
A fragrant mixture of fresh fruits to
start. Citrus accentuates fruit in the
middle, well balanced by biscuity malt.
Clean, dry finish.

# Flying Fish

1940 Olney Avenue, Cherry Hill,
New Jersey 08003, **USA**
www.flyingfish.com

Flying Fish Brewing began
worldwide and then went local.
It started out as a "virtual
brewery" on the Internet before
establishing itself as a distinctly
regional brewery in 1996, now
serving a 100-mile (160-km)
radius around its South Jersey
home. The brewery recently
increased capacity, with plans to
widen the range of beers on offer.

### Belgian Style Dubbel

DOUBLE 7% ABV
Chocolate mingled with dark fruit, and a
pleasant whiff of alcohol. Finishes on the
sweet side of dry.

### ESB Ale

EXTRA SPECIAL BITTER 5.5% ABV
Malt-accented, rich with caramel
and fruit character, and with an
underlying nuttiness. Hops are
American, but restrained.

# Forstner

Dorfstrasse 52, A-8401 Kalsdorf
bei Graz, **AUSTRIA**
www.hofbraeu.at

One of the more adventurous
new brewers, Gerhard Forstner
has recently made inroads into
brewing Belgian and American-
style ales. His brewery is in an
old farmhouse building that has
also served as a school. Some of
his beers are endorsed by the
Slow Food movement and are
sold at Slow Food festivals.

## Styrian Ale

BITTER ALE 5.6% ABV
Very dark burgundy; roasty and fruity
(grapefruit?) aromas; slightly tart and
very refreshing, with a medium bitterness.

## Triple 22

BELGIAN STYLE TRIPLE 9.5% ABV
Copper, with firm head and aroma of
pawpaw and mango. Sweet and full-
bodied; spicy and bitter finish.

# Friedenfels

Schlossbrauerei Friedenfels,
Gemmingenstr. 33, 95688
Friedenfels, **GERMANY**
www.schlossbrauerei-friedenfels.de

The brewery is situated in the
southern part of the largest
forest in Europe, between
Oberpfälzer Wald and
Fichtelgebirge. Friedenfels is the
leading brewery of the region.

**BREWING SECRET** The pure springs of
the national park have helped Friedenfels
to produce excellent beers for more than
100 years.

### Friedenfelser Pils Leicht
**LIGHT BEER 2.8% ABV**
This reduced-alcohol beer is golden and
on the dry side, with aromas of fine hops
in the finish.

### Friedenfelser Weizen Leicht
**LIGHT WHEAT BEER 2.7% ABV**
This light beer is fermented in the bottle.
Its taste is a mixture of bitter hops and
sweet barley and wheat – typical of
the style.

# Freistädter

Promenade 7, A-4240 Freistadt,
**AUSTRIA**
www.freistaedter-bier.at

The town of Freistadt lies close
to Austria's border with the
Czech Republic, and its brewery
is owned by the townspeople.
Since 1777 every owner of a
building inside the old city walls
automatically owns a certain
number of shares of the brewery;
those shares can be sold only
along with the building itself.

### Rauchbier
**SMOKED LAGER 5.3% ABV**
Pale amber, with a smoky nose; dry and
aromatic, with a nice balance of smoked
malt and hops.

### Ratsherrn Trunk
**EXPORT 5.1% ABV**
A firm head and a full body. Low hop
bitterness, with a hint of grass in
the aftertaste.

# Füchschen

Ratinger Str. 28, 40213 Düsseldorf,
**GERMANY**
www.fuechschen.de

Altbier has been a favoured brew
at Füchschen since 1848. The
fourth generation of the family
is in charge. There have been
some changes since 1995,
including the installation of
new brewing equipment.

**BREWING SECRET** The Düsseldorf
carnival in February is a good
opportunity to sample the altbier.

## Füchschen Alt
**ALTBIER 4.5% ABV**
Dark mahogany in colour, this typical
Düsseldorfer is malty with a very
intense aroma of hops. Slightly
carbonated, and fresh.

## Silberfüchsen
**WHEAT BEER 5.4% ABV**
A northern-style wheat beer, less sweet
than its Bavarian counterpart. Smooth,
fruity, and sparkling.

# Fuller's

Chiswick Lane South, London,
W4 2QB **ENGLAND**
www.fullers.co.uk

London's last remaining
traditional family brewer,
Fuller's has been based at the
historic Griffin Brewery near
the River Thames in Chiswick
since 1845. Brewing on the site,
however, goes back 350 years.
Despite its global prominence,
Fuller's retains a small company
spirit and formidably energetic
outlook. Its beers have received
countless awards, notably
the Campaign For Real Ale
Champion Beer of Britain,
which it has won five times.

### London Pride
BITTER **4.1**% ABV
A fruity sweet malt nose and a floral
spiced hop presence with marmalade
undercurrents.

### ESB
EXTRA SPECIAL BITTER **5.5**% ABV
Complex aromas, with the house-style
orange fruit complementing tangy hops
and roasted malt.

# Full Sail

506 Columbia Street, Hood River,
Oregon 97031, **USA**
www.fullsailbrewing.com

Full Sail represents much that
is new in American brewing.
Founded in 1987, it became
employee-owned in 1999, and
its beers reflect an independent
nature. The core brands (Amber,
IPA, and Pale Ale) reach a wide
audience in 15 western states.

**BREWING SECRET** The brewery also
offers seasonals that bear the LTD (Living
the Dream) label and a bolder series of
Brewmaster's Reserve beers throughout
the year.

## Amber
AMBER ALE 5.5% ABV
Citrus and spice, quickly balanced by
underlying sweetness. Seamless through
to a clean finish.

## Session Lager
US LAGER 5.1% ABV
Designed as a throwback to beer
produced before Prohibition, with
appropriately retro packaging. Clean
and malt-accented.

# Fürstenberg

Postplatz 1-4, 78166
Donaueschingen, **GERMANY**
www.fuerstenberg.de

Count Heinrich I von
Fürstenberg was granted the
right to brew beer in 1283, but
it was not until 300 years later
that a proper brewery was built.
Fürstenberg was a major
brewery by the beginning
of the 20th century.

**BREWING SECRET** The beers are made
with water from the Black Forest and
yeast from Donaueschingen.

### Fürstenberg Gold
LAGER **4.9%** ABV
Smooth, with few aromas of hops. This
clear golden beer is a bit sweeter than
the usual lager.

### Fürstenberg Hefe Dunkel
DUNKEL **5.4%** ABV
Chestnut in colour, and sparkling;
harmonious with a malty aroma and
light caramel sweetness, yet strong
in the mouth.

# Fürstlichen Ellingen

Schloss-Strasse 19, 91792 Ellingen, **GERMANY**
www.fuerst-carl.de

Owner Carl Friedrich Fürst von Wrede is a direct descendant of Napoleon's field marshal Carl Philipp, Prince of Wrede. The brewery opposite his castle in Ellingen was founded in 1690, but the brewing history of Ellingen is certainly older. The beer has been called Fürst Carl for about 200 years.

### Fürst Carl Josefi Bock

BOCK 7% ABV
A creamy, malty, and full-bodied beer, with a velvet and silky texture.

### Fürst Carl Urhell

LAGER 4.6% ABV
The clear yellow colour is typical for a lager; the taste is pleasant and not too dry, with very little sweetness.

# Galbraith's

2 Mt Eden Road, Mt Eden,
Auckland, **NEW ZEALAND**
www.alehouse.co.nz

Located in a former library, New
Zealand's first real ale brewpub is
best known for its home-brewed
English style ales – all served by
hand pump. Visitors can also
enjoy an excellent Abbey-style
ale and a couple of flavoursome
lagers, as well as a fine range
of imports and craft beers from
other New Zealand brewers.

### Bellringers Bitter

ENGLISH BEST BITTER **4.5**% ABV
Copper coloured ale with a biscuity,
toffee-like palate, plenty of earthy hops,
and an appetizingly dry finish.

### Bob Hudson's Bitter

ENGLISH BITTER **4**% ABV
A full-flavoured session bitter very much
in the vein of the English pale ale
Timothy Taylor's Landlord.

# Gayant

63 Faubourg de Paris,
59500 Douai, **FRANCE**
www.brasseurs-gayant.com

Established in 1919, this
independent, family-owned
brewery has always embraced
and pioneered new styles of
brewing, from ales made
using the top-fermentation
technique, to Celta, the first
non-alcoholic beer.

**BREWING SECRET** Brasseurs de Gayant
brews the strongest beer in France, called
Bière du Démon (12% ABV).

## La Goudale
ALE **7.2% ABV**
Golden, dense, and full of malty aromas,
with a slight bitterness imbued by the
Flemish hops.

## Amadeus
WHEAT BEER **4.5% ABV**
Cloudy and pale yellow, this is a light
and refreshing beer, with aromas of citrus
fruit and coriander.

# Gilde

Hildesheimer Str. 132,
Hanover, **GERMANY**
www.gildebrau.de

It was about 500 years ago that
Cord Broyhan presented his beer
to the people of Hanover.
*Broyhan* – a pale style of wheat
beer – was popular for centuries
in the city. Gilde, Hanover's
longest-surviving brewery,
now owned by InBev, was
founded in 1870.

**BREWING SECRET** A modern version
of *broyhan* is exported to the USA.

## Ratskeller Premium Pils
PILSNER 4.9% ABV
A dry, golden-yellow pilsner; full-
bodied, typical bitterness of hops,
and a nice finish.

## Lindener Special
EXPORT 5.1% ABV
The most successful export beer of
Niedersachsen has a golden colour and
tastes pleasant with smooth yeast-flower
flavours in the mouth.

# Girardin

Lindeberg 10-12,
1700 Sint-Ulriks-Kapelle, **BELGIUM**
www.brouwerijgirardin.com

As rural as you can get, Girardin
is still very much a farm and
brewery, and this authentic
lambic brewer and gueuze
blender has no time for curious
visitors. If, however, you come
simply to stock up on lambic –
as the locals and other blenders
do – the brewers will gladly
help you to their citrusy,
spontaneously fermented brews.

### Faro Girardin
BLENDED LAMBIC 5% ABV
Caramel, meaty, and woody aromas;
slight sour edge around the caramel.
Filtered, as the yeast would wreak
havoc with sugars from the syrup.

### Girardin Fond Gueuze
GUEUZE 5% ABV
This delectable unfiltered gueuze has
a marked grapefruit flavour.

# Glaab

Frankfurter Str. 9, 63500
Seligenstadt, **GERMANY**
www.glaabsbraeu.de

For more than 250 years this
brewery has been owned by the
Glaab family. It was founded in
1744 and became known for its
wide variety of beers and for
Vitamalz, the biggest German
brand of pure malt drinks. The
company is the only private
brewery in the Offenbach region,
to the south of Frankfurt.

### 1744

KELLERBIER **5.3%** ABV
This cloudy, amber-coloured beer is
Glaab's youngest product. The taste
of fine malt is typical.

### Dunkles

DUNKEL **5.3%** ABV
Clear amber-coloured beer in which the
light bitterness of hops is prominent.
A great dunkel with a nice malty finish.

# Goose Island

1800 West Fulton Street, Chicago,
Illinois 60612, **USA**
www.gooseisland.com

This brewery's extensive range
reflects the MBA (Master of Beer
Appreciation) Programme that it
established shortly after opening
as a brewpub in 1988. When
Goose Island built its production
brewery in 1995, brewmaster
Greg Hall would launch dozens
of styles during the course of a
year. Goose Island still operates
the original pub on Clybourn and
another near Wrigley Field, and
both still offer an "MBA" (actually
a kind of loyalty card!).

### India Pale Ale
INDIA PALE ALE **5.9**% ABV
Pineapple and grapefruit, full of hop
flavour, with a fruit and malt backbone
balancing the bitterness.

### 312 Urban Wheat
US WHEAT BEER **4.2**% ABV
Typically unfiltered and hazy, with
a citrusy, almost sweet, hop nose that
announces it is American. Tart, fruity,
with underlying creaminess.

# Gourmet-bryggeriet

Bytoften 10-12,
DK-4000 Roskilde, **DENMARK**
www.gourmetbryggeriet.dk

One of the largest
microbreweries in Denmark,
"The Gourmet Brewery" creates
speciality beers that are designed
to be paired with food. The
brewery's partner is a trained
chef who works together with
a local restaurant to create
recipes that are attached to
66cl bottles for sharing. The
company recently acquired the
Ølfabrikken Brewery.

### Ølfabrikken Porter
PORTER 7.5% ABV
Black as the night, with a thick head of
foam. Intense body with coffee, chocolate,
and liquorice notes.

### Gourmetbryggeriet Bock
DOPPELBOCK 7.2% ABV
Deep reddish in colour, with a heavy
aroma of malt and caramel backing
up the strong body.

# Great Divide

2201 Arapahoe Street, Denver, Colorado 80205, **USA**
www.greatdivide.com

Opened in 1994, Great Divide Brewing quickly earned a reputation for carefully balanced beers. Its ales have grown bigger (in strength and hop character), and the brewery's reputation has grown, but its beers still retain that delicate equilibrium. The brewery is a short walk from Coors Field, home of the Rockies baseball team.

### Hibernation Ale

OLD ALE 8.1% ABV

A complex, earthy nose packed with chocolate, roasted nuts, and freshly baked molasses cookies – flavours just keep emerging.

### Titan IPA

INDIA PALE ALE 6.8% ABV

Balanced, in a big way, with plenty of caramel-sweet body to match the piney, grapefruity hops throughout.

# Great Lakes

2516 Market Avenue, Cleveland,
Ohio 44113, **USA**
www.greatlakesbrewing.com

Selling its beer across a growing
region, this brewery has been an
industry leader in tracking the
quality of its beer on retailers'
shelves. Its brewing complex
always merits a visit. The original
1988 brewpub, sits across from
the production brewery, which
came online in 1998. Visitors
are directed to the taproom's
striking Tiger Mahogany bar
and shown bullet holes reputedly
made by Eliot Ness, the
Prohibition agent who brought
down gangster Al Capone.

### Edmund Fitzgerald Porter
**PORTER 5.8% ABV**
Perfectly balanced, chocolate-mocha
throughout, delightful fresh quality,
and a dry coffee finish.

### Eliot Ness
**VIENNA LAGER 6.2% ABV**
Bold and hoppy in the Vienna style, with
creamy, nutty maltiness and brisk
hoppiness nicely balanced.

# Green Flash

1430 Vantage Court, Vista,
California 92081, **USA**
www.greenflashbrew.com

Green Flash refers to a rare light
phenomenon that lasts only
seconds at sunrise or sunset over
water. Green seems appropriate
for a brewery gaining a national
reputation for its hop-accented
beers, although brewer Chuck
Silva has proved adept at a wide
range of styles.

### West Coast IPA

INDIA PALE ALE **7**% ABV
Northwest hops balanced on a solid malt
base. Earthy, floral, citrusy, piney,
grapefruity, and bitter.

### Nut Brown Ale

BROWN ALE **5.5**% ABV
Deep brown, with nuts and cocoa
from the outset, and more chocolate
and caramel on the palate. Subdued,
earthy hops.

# Greene King

Bury St Edmunds, Suffolk,
IP33 1QT **ENGLAND**
www.greeneking.co.uk

After more than 200 years,
Greene King has developed into
a formidable and dynamic force
in the British brewing industry.
Benjamin Greene opened his
brewery in 1799 and it merged with
the rival King Brewery in 1887.
The company has in recent
years acquired several of its
competitors – namely, Morland,
Ruddles, Ridley's, and Hardy &
Hanson – and closed them amid
some controversy. Belhaven of
Dunbar was another recent
acquisition, it being bought
up in 2005.

### Abbot Ale
STRONG BITTER 5% ABV
A biscuit malt and spicy hop aroma, with a
tangy and bittersweet fruit and malt palate.

### IPA
INDIA PALE ALE 3.6% ABV
Distinctly copper-coloured, with a clean,
fresh hop savouriness and subtle,
sweetish malty nose.

# Grünbach

Kellerberg 2, 85461 Bockhorn,
**GERMANY**
www.schlossbrauerei-gruenbach.de

Grünbach has had a host of
owners, including the famous
Paulaner and Erdinger
breweries. Alexander Noll
is currently at the helm.

**BREWING SECRET** Grünbach's Benno
Scharl wheat beer carries the name
of an 18th-century Bavarian master
brewer who wrote an influential textbook
on brewing techniques.

## Altweizen Gold
**WHEAT BEER 5.3% ABV**
Clear golden and finely balanced between
yeast and carbonic acid, with a lightly
sparkling, dry freshness.

## Benno Scharl
**WHEAT BEER 5.3% ABV**
Yellow, and clouded with yeast, Benno
Scharl tastes mild and sweet, pleasant
and well balanced.

# Guinness

St James's Gate, Dublin 8, **IRELAND**
www.guinness.com

When you can make a virtue out of the time it takes to pour a pint – 119.5 seconds to be precise – you know you have no ordinary beer in your hands. Guinness defines stout, Ireland, and Irishness, but it is also inextricably linked with innovation in physics, chemistry, packaging, and advertising. 250 years after young Arthur Guinness's first mash, it is brewed in 50 countries worldwide and enjoyed in 150.

### Guinness Original
STOUT 4.2% ABV
The packaged version's coffee and cream aroma highlights fruit, chocolate, and some late hoppiness.

### Foreign Extra Stout
SPECIAL STOUT 7.5% ABV
Leafy hop aroma, with burnt toast, rich malt, bitter coffee, and liquorice flavours ripening effortlessly.

# Haake-Beck

Am Deich 18/19, 28365
Bremen, **GERMANY**
www.haake-beck.de

Founded in 1826, the Haake-Beck brewery is one of the most famous in northern Germany. Milestones in the company's history include the creation of Haake-Beck Kräusen Pils and the first Maibock in 1950. It is part of the InBev stable today.

**BREWING SECRET** Haake-Beck's sister is the famous Beck's label, which is exported by InBev around the world.

### Haake-Beck 12
**EXPORT 5% ABV**
This is a new Haake-Beck. A harmonious, golden beer, with a level of sweetness that is often liked by women drinkers.

### Edel Hell
**LAGER 4.7% ABV**
A mild alternative to the pilsner: not so dry, a little bit sweet, and golden like a typical lager.

# Haandbryggeriet

Thornegaten 39,
N-3015 Drammen, **NORWAY**
www.haandbryggeriet.net

This small brewery is known for its hand-made brews and for keeping Norwegian brewing traditions alive. Housed in a 200-year-old wooden building, it is run by volunteers, and experimentation is encouraged.

**BREWING SECRET** As well as using old oak wine barrels, they are now ageing beer in former Akevitt spirit casks.

## Dark Force
WHEAT STOUT 9% ABV
Uses wheat and dark roasted malts and house wheat yeast. High hop aroma and ample bitterness.

## Norwegian Wood
TRADITIONAL ALE 6.5% ABV
Made from naturally smoked Munich, Crystal, and chocolate malts; spiced with locally gathered juniper twigs and berries.

# Hacker-Pschorr

Hochstr. 75, 81541 München,
**GERMANY**
www.hacker-pschorr.de

Hacker-Pschorr is one of the
most traditional breweries in
Munich, and its restaurant is
a tourist attraction, especially
during the Oktoberfest. Beer
production was mentioned for
the first time here in 1417.

**BREWING SECRET** The Purity Law and
principles of long lagering are followed;
there are no preservatives or additives.

## Anno 1417
**KELLERBIER 5.5% ABV**
Naturally cloudy, unfiltered, with a dull
golden colour. Low carbonic acid makes
it very smooth.

## Superior
**MÜNCHNER SPECIAL 6% ABV**
The clear, amber-coloured Superior is
based on an old recipe and has a malty,
aromatic taste, without too many hops.
Highly drinkable.

# Hair of the Dog

4509 Southeast 23rd Avenue,
Portland, Oregon 97202, **USA**
www.hairofthedog.com

Chef-turned-brewer Alan Sprints
founded this tiny cult brewery in
1994. His first ale, Adam, was
brewed in the Adambier style of
Dortmund in Germany, and
based on the research of beer
writer Fred Eckhardt.

**BREWING SECRET** Every bottle carries
a batch number. Check the website to
match it to brewing and bottling dates.

## Adam
STRONG ALE 10% ABV
Rich and complex, with dark fruits,
bread, chocolate, smoked peat, and more,
all cleverly unified.

## Fred
STRONG ALE 10% ABV
Named after Eckhardt, this beer defies
categorization. Dark fruits and juicy
ones, spices and hops – impossible
to summarize.

# Hakusekikan

5251-1 Hirukawa Tahara,
Nagatsugawa, Gifu 509-8301, **JAPAN**
www.hakusekikan-beer.jp

One of Japan's most distinctive
breweries, Hakusekikan pushes
the envelope of possible beer
styles. Head brewer Satoshi Niwa
is brilliant and imaginative,
experimenting with wild beers
using airborne yeast, while also
making use of long fermentation
times, barrel ageing, and other
methods to produce truly
distinctive beers.

### Super Vintage
STRONG ALE 14.3% ABV
Astonishingly fruity and complex beer,
yet boasts a surprisingly dry finish.
Permanently on tap at Beer Club Popeye
in Tokyo.

### Smoked Pale Ale
PALE ALE 5% ABV
A session pale ale given just a hint of
smoked malt, with the smoky flavour
appearing only in the finish.

# Hambleton

Holme-on-Swale, North Yorkshire,
YO7 4JE **ENGLAND**
www.hambletonales.co.uk

A million-pound investment has
resulted in a completely new
brewery for Hambleton, with
state-of-the-art bottling facilities.
Innovation has been at the heart
of the operation since 1991, as
evident in the label designs and
bespoke brewing equipment.
Several awards, including one
for a gluten-free range, have
been well deserved.

## Stallion
BITTER 4.2% ABV
For some, a true Yorkshire bitter, with its
malty character, nuttiness, and enhanced
hopping rate.

## Nightmare
PORTER 5% ABV
An extra-stout porter that uses a
combination of four malts for a massively
complex flavour.

# Harpoon

306 Northern Avenue, Boston,
Massachusetts 02210, **USA**
www.harpoonbrewery.com

This brewery, with major
facilities in Boston and Vermont,
has tapped into speciality-beer-
drinkers' affection for hops, with
its flagship IPA accounting for
60 per cent of sales. However, its
wheat-based UFO has recently
been the fastest-growing brand,
and its 100 Barrel Series of
one-offs guarantees there's
always something new.

### IPA

INDIA PALE ALE **5.9**% ABV

Floral at the outset; zestful citrus aromas.
More hops in the flavour, biscuit-like
palate, subdued bitterness at the end.

### Munich Dark

DUNKEL **5.5**% ABV

Rich, almost sweet, with hints of toast,
then chocolate. Restrained hops and
a long, smooth finish.

# Harvey's

Lewes, East Sussex, BN7 2AH
**ENGLAND**
www.harveys.org.uk

The seventh generation of John Harvey's descendants are still involved in this prime example of Victorian Gothic-style brewery grandeur. The tower and brewhouse dominate the skyline, and the fermenting rooms and cellars remain structurally unaltered, although they now house a modern plant with equipment that has increased production enormously.

## Blue Label

PALE ALE **3.6**% ABV
Deliciously full-bodied though fairly low in alcohol, with a whiff of leafy hop and sweet malt counterbalance.

## Armada Ale

BEST BITTER **4.5**% ABV
Amber coloured, with a well-balanced combination of fruit and hops on the palate.

# Harviestoun

Alva, Clackmannanshire,
FK12 5DQ **SCOTLAND**
www.harviestoun-brewery.co.uk

The brewers of Harviestoun say
they can't pretend it's a job – it's
their work, but also their play
and their passion. Curiosity
towards flavours and aromas
wrung from natural ingredients
was the brewery's mission in
1985, when the business was
originally set up, and a move to
a purpose-built plant with fresh
investment has resulted
in national accolades.

## Bitter & Twisted
BITTER 4.2% ABV
Ripe grapefruit and lemon-influenced
hop aromas are anchored by a
distinct maltiness.

## Schiehallion
PREMIUM LAGER 4.8% ABV
Cask lager, brewed with Bavarian hops
for a delightful nose. A rigid maltiness
prevails throughout.

# Hawkshead

Staveley, Cumbria,
LA8 9LR **ENGLAND**
www.hawksheadbrewery.co.uk

The focus at Hawkshead is on traditional beer styles that have been given a modern twist. A new 20-barrel (3,200-litre) brewhouse was fitted out in 2006 – an integral feature is a farm gate for leaning on contemplatively. The brewery's public beer hall, where award-winning ales are served, is a magnificent showcase for the beers and their provenance.

## Hawkshead Red

RED ALE 4.2% ABV
A bittersweet red ale, malty and spicy on the palate, with juicy, woody aromas.

## Hawkshead Gold

BEST BITTER 4.4% ABV
Hoppy and uncompromisingly bitter, with complex fruit flavours from its English and American hop blend.

# Herold

262 72 Březnice, **CZECH REPUBLIC**
www.heroldbeer.com

The town's Baroque castle is fully restored, and its attached brewery continues to produce pilsner-style beers in a traditional, hand-crafted manner to a "small is beautiful" philosophy. The range includes wheat beers and Bohemian Black Lager.

**BREWING SECRET** Open fermenters, home-drawn water, and resident maltings accentuate its heritage.

## Bohemian Black Lager

DARK LAGER **4.1% ABV**
A schwarzbier-type lager; bitter chocolate flavours, plus a little malty sweetness, and a long, dry, slightly smoky finish.

## Premium Bohemian Lager

PREMIUM LAGER **5.1% ABV**
Full-bodied, yet softly textured, with a classic creamy malt veil and late hop dryness.

# Herrngiersdorf

Schlossallee 5, 84097 Herrngiersdorf,
**GERMANY**
www.schlossbrauerei-
herrngiersdorf.de

Herrngiersdorf is situated
between Regensburg and
Landhut, in the middle of
Niederbayern. With more than
875 years of history behind it,
this is the oldest private brewery
in the world. It has been owned
by the Pausinger family since
1899. Since 1995 the sixth
generation of the family has
been managing it.

### Sündenbock
BOCK 7.3% ABV
A typical dark doppelbock with
a light taste of caramel; very full-bodied
and sweet in the finish.

### Publiner
DUNKEL 4.9% ABV
This beer is very dark and has a strong
taste, with very roasty malt aromas
and light bitters of hops. (The Irish
would love it...)

# High Falls

445 St. Paul Street, Rochester,
New York 14605, **USA**
www.highfalls.com

High Falls is still brewing old-style Genesee beers on the site where they have been made since 1878. It also makes the JW Dundee family of beers for the traditional ale market.

**BREWING SECRET** High Falls is one of the largest and oldest continuously operating breweries in the US.

### Genesee Cream Ale
CREAM ALE **4.9**% ABV
Pale, faintly sweet, with roast corn flavours; smooth and easy to drink.

### JW Dundee's IPA
INDIA PALE ALE **6.3**% ABV
A seasonal summer beer. Relatively sweet caramel character, with more bitterness than flavour from its hops. Crisp finish.

# Hite

640, Yeongdeungpo-Dong,
Yeongdeungpo, Seoul,
**SOUTH KOREA**
www.hite.com

Founded in 1933 as Chosun
Breweries, Hite is Korea's leading
brewer, with 60 per cent of local
sales. Carlsberg is a substantial
investor in the brewery. The
present production at Hite
amounts to approximately
seven million hectolitres (150
million gallons) per annum.
The company also makes a
rice-based wine.

### Hite
LAGER 4.5% ABV
Golden in colour, Hite is a light,
easy drinking beer – with an aroma
of bubblegum.

### Prime Max
LAGER 4.5% ABV
Pale orange in colour; with a sweetcorn
aroma, it has hints of biscuit and
citrus fruits.

# Hoegaarden

Stoopkensstraat 46,
B3320 Hoegaarden, **BELGIUM**
www.inbev.com

Although this is now a brand
in the portfolio of brewing giant
InBev, it is the lifeblood and
spirit of Pierre Celis, Belgium's
preeminent brewing
revolutionary, that still haunts
this brewery. Proof of this came
in 2007, when InBev's moguls
wanted to close the plant: fate,
however, obliged them to reverse
their decision.

### Hoegaarden Wit

**WITBIER 4.9% ABV**

From as early as the 18th century,
the town of Hoegaarden was importing
blue Curaçao oranges. The peel was
mixed with coriander seeds, and, as the
rich soil of the area yielded lots of wheat,
a very distinct, fruity, and spicy style
of beer evolved.

# Hofbräu München

Hofbräuallee 1, 81829 München,
**GERMANY**
www.hofbraeuhaus.com

The Hofbräuhaus in Munich
is a very famous restaurant,
frequented by visitors from
around the world. It was
founded in 1607 by Maximilian I,
Duke of Bavaria. The linked
brewery is situated in Riem,
outside of the city.

**BREWING SECRET** The water used to
brew Hofbräu is drawn from a depth of
150m (490ft).

### Hofbräu Original
MÜNCHNER HELLES **5.1%** ABV
This clear golden beer is refreshing
and dry, with a harmonious balance
of malt and hops.

### Hofbräu Dunkel
DUNKEL **5.5%** ABV
This is the oldest type of Bavarian beer,
dark amber in colour, and full of fine
flavour and enticing malt aromas.

# Hogs Back

Tongham, Surrey, GU10 1DE
**ENGLAND**
www.hogsback.co.uk

Established in 1992, the Hogs Back brewhouse takes up part of an 18th-century farm. Steady expansion, extensions to storage facilities, and re-equipping the fermenting room have continued since, and many awards have been gathered along the way.

**BREWERY SECRETS** "Late hops" are added at the end of the boil, contributing additional fragrance to the beer.

### Traditional English Ale / TEA
BEST BITTER **4.2% ABV**
Well-crafted, with delicate fruity aromas, some bittersweet malt flavouring, and a long dry finish.

### Hogs Back Bitter
BITTER 3.7% ABV
A biscuit-influenced session bitter, with a fragrantly aromatic citrus fruit and light malt afterglow.

# Holden's

Woodsetton, Dudley, West Midlands, DY1 4LW **ENGLAND**
www.holdensbrewery.co.uk

Third and fourth-generation family members are very much involved in the Holden's business, which started life in the 1920s with a brewpub, before expanding next door into a neatly tiled brewery on two floors.

**BREWING SECRET** The mild uses a mix of amber malt, caramalt, and black malt, along with Fuggles hops.

### Holden's Golden
BITTER **3.9%** ABV
Fuggles hops and Maris Otter malt combine in this medium-bodied, straw-hued pale ale.

### Black Country Mild
MILD **3.7%** ABV
Bold chestnut red, with nutty biscuit notes and wrappings of chocolate, caramel, and earthy hops.

# Holt

Cheetham, Manchester,
M3 1JD **ENGLAND**
www.joseph-holt.com

A family business survivor in
an increasingly corporate sector,
Holt's admits – with some pride
– to being unashamedly old-
fashioned. That does not mean
backward-looking, however, and
its well-structured projects and
clear vision have brought steady
expansion to the brewery and
to its portfolio of 127 pubs.

### Holt 1849

BEST BITTER 4.5% ABV

A 150-year anniversary ale, with a
vibrant and generous celebratory hop
flavour to match.

### Holt Bitter

BITTER 4% ABV

Spicy hops dominate the aroma with tart
fruitiness tempered by biscuit malt and
bittersweet fruit.

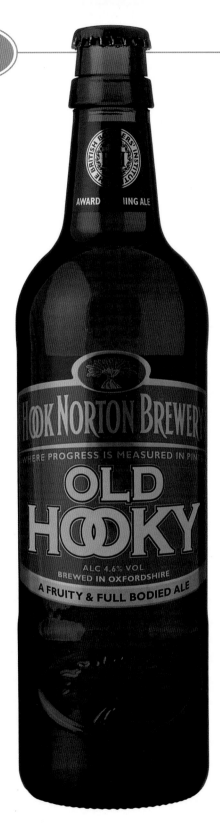

# Hook Norton

Banbury, Oxfordshire, OX15 5NY
**ENGLAND**
www.hooky.co.uk

A particularly striking example of a Victorian tower brewery, Hook Norton is partly powered by steam, via a series of belts, cogs, and shafts. Drays pulled by shire horses deliver to local pubs, further demonstrating how the brewery likes to preserve traditional practices. While doing this, Hook Norton also produces some of the country's most outstanding ales.

### Old Hooky

STRONG BITTER **4.6**% ABV
Beautifully poised, with a piquant, fruity nature and malt character rounding off a bitter finish.

### Hooky Bitter

BITTER **3.6**% ABV
Subtly hoppy on the nose, then malt and fruit appear, before a returning hop finish.

# COTSWOLDS, ENGLAND

The village of Hook Norton in north Oxfordshire is the perfect base for any visitor exploring the Cotswolds, and it is also convenient for the city of Oxford. For the traveller, three of the village's pubs – the Sun, the Pear Tree and the Gate Hangs High – all offer accommodation.

**1** DAY 1: **HOOK NORTON BREWERY**
This is a near-perfect example of a Victorian tower brewery. It is still powered by a steam engine, and the making of Hook Norton's beers is a tactile, aural, and visual experience. Only the finest malted barley is used in the mash tun, and this needs to be manually removed when the wort is drained off the grist. The seemingly magical transformation of turning sweet wort into alcohol takes place in the brewery's hard-working open fermenters. A horse-drawn dray still delivers beer to local pubs. The Visitor Centre is open from Monday to Saturday, though tours of the brewery must be booked beforehand via the website. The tour is followed by some sampling of Hook Norton beer. *Brewery Lane, Hook Norton (www.hooky.co.uk)*

**2** DAY 2: **WYCHWOOD BREWERY**
The drive from Hook Norton to Witney takes in some glorious countryside, and at the end of the journey is the Wychwood Brewery. Tours of the brewery can be booked online. They last for two hours and go through the brewing process for Wychwood and Brakspear beers, from raw ingredients to the finished product. The tour takes in Brakspear's famous "Double Drop system" fermenting vessels. *Eagle Maltings, The Crofts, Witney (www.wychwood.co.uk)*

**3** **THE KING'S HEAD INN**
Before returning to Hook Norton, pass by Cotswold Brewing (www.cotswold brewing company.com) at Foscot. Unusually for a British micro, brewer Richard Keene makes continental-style lagers. With a meandering stream at its side, the King's Head Inn, at nearby Bledington, is the perfect place to drink a glass of Cotswold Brewing's beer. *The King's Head Inn, The Green, Bledington (www.thekingsheadinn.net)*

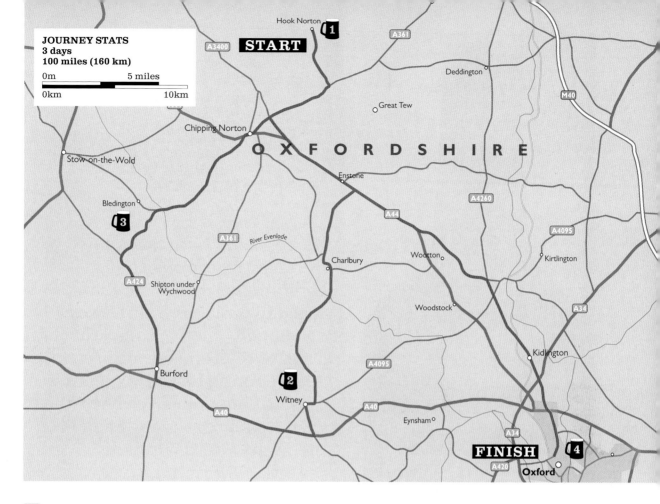

## DAY 3: OXFORD

The third day of the trail offers a chance to sample some of the fabulous pubs in the historical city of Oxford – a place where good beer, culture, and a convivial atmosphere sit cosily together.

### The Bear

Small and friendly, The Bear is on a narrow lane between Christ Church and Oriel colleges. It claims to be the oldest pub in Oxford, and is built on the site of a former bear-fighting pit. The walls are decorated by a collection of 5,000 ties. *6 Alfred Street, Oxford*

### King's Arms

The King's Arms sits at the end of Broad Street, which is famous for its colleges and bookshops. The large pub is a warren of rooms and is much loved by locals and students. *40 Holywell Street, Oxford*

### Turf Tavern

Hard to find but worth the search, the Turf Tavern is built on the only remaining part of the city wall. It sells a fabulous collection of British beers.
***Bath Place, Holywell, Oxford (www.theturftavern.co.uk)***

### Eagle & Child

Close to Oxford's dreaming spires and the Ashmolean museum of art and architecture, Eagle & Child was a frequent haunt of writers JRR Tolkein and CS Lewis, who were part of a literary group in the 1930s and 40s called the *Inklings*.
*49 St Giles, Oxford*

# Hop Back

Downton, Salisbury, Wiltshire,
SP5 3HU **ENGLAND**
www.hopback.co.uk

Having soon outgrown its
humble 1980s pub-cellar
beginnings at the Wyndham
Arms in Salisbury, Hop Back
developed and expanded through
a series of premises for brewing
and drinking its beers, picking
up significant awards along the
way. At the core of the range is
the multi-award-winning
Summer Lightning.

### Summer Lightning
STRONG BITTER 5% ABV

Intensely bitter, with a grassy, fresh,
hoppy aroma and some malt lingering
on the palate.

### Crop Circle
BITTER 4.2% ABV

Cleverly blended aroma and bittering
hops combine with corn nuances for
a delicate fruity crispness.

# Hopworks / HUB

2944 SE Powell Boulevard, Portland,
Oregon 97202, **USA**
www.hopworksbeer.com

Hopworks Urban Brewery is the
first brewery in Portland to offer
only organic beers, part of its
commitment to "green culture".
HUB's founder-brewmaster
Christian Ettinger made
Portland's first organic beers.

**BREWING SECRET** HUB fires its
brewing kettle with bio-diesel fuel.

## Velvet ESB
SPECIAL BITTER **5.2%** ABV
A session ale by American standards;
rich in caramel, soft on the palate, with
signature hop character throughout.

## Organic IPA
INDIA PALE ALE **6.6%** ABV
Fresh hop aromas – pine, grapefruit,
lemon zest. Hop flavours, bitterness
matched by bright malt character.

# Hue

243 Nguyen Sinh Cung
Hue City, **VIETNAM**

The Hue Brewery is based in Hue City, the old capital of Vietnam, on the banks of the famous Perfume River in central Vietnam. Carlsberg – which entered Vietnam in 1993 with the acquisition of a 60 per cent stake in South East Asia Brewery, based in the north of the country – now has a 50 per cent share in the Hue Brewery.

## Hue

LAGER 5% ABV

A yellow corn colour with a thin white head, and the body seems somewhat thin too. It is an easy-drinking beer, without surprises and a nose with hints of toast. Not much complexity, but a refresher nonetheless.

# Huvila

Puistokatu 4, FI-57100,
Savonlinna, **FINLAND**
www.panimoravintolahuvila.fi

This craft brewery, making
British-style ales, *sideri* (cider),
and *sahti*, is located in
Savonlinna, a popular tourist
area in the Lake Saimaa area.
The complex offers good food
at the brewery-restaurant
Huvila, bed and breakfast, live
music, brewery tours, and a
brewing school.

**BREWING SECRET** All of Huvila's
products are unfiltered.

### Huvila Porter
PORTER 5.5% ABV
English roasted malts give a strong
coffee-like, roasted aroma with a hint
of chocolate.

### Huvila ESB
STRONG BITTER 5.2% ABV
Robustly hopped with a fruity and floral
aroma, complex flavours, and a long and
bitter aftertaste.

# Hydes

46 Moss Lane West, Manchester,
M15 5PH **ENGLAND**
www.hydesbrewery.com

Hydes is another of those remarkable family-owned breweries that has carved out a niche in its home region. Hydes Original has persevered with the same recipe and exacting standards that were applied on day one – back in 1863. The business continues to face the future with enthusiasm and in confident style.

### Hydes Original

BITTER **3.8**% ABV
A northwest classic: copper-coloured, full-bodied, with a distinctive bittersweet flavour.

### Dark Mild

MILD **3.5**% ABV
A fruit and malt nose and complex flavourings that meander through berry fruits, malt, and chocolate.

# Ilzer Sörgyár

Ilzer Sörgyár Rt., 2200,
Monor, **HUNGARY**
www.ilzer.hu

Located 35 km (22 miles) south
of Budapest, this brewery was
founded in the early 1990s. Its
range of brews now includes
Alt Bayersicher Dunkel, a dark
wheat beer; Diet, a beer that
is low in sugar; and a kosher
beer called Shalom.

**BREWING SECRET** Ilzer developed and
brewed the first Hungarian wheat beer.

### Ilzer Hefeweissbier
**WHEAT BEER 5% ABV**
Cloudy yellow, with a wispy white head.
Hints of banana and spice give way to a
citrusy finish.

### Ilzer Roggen Rozs Sör
**RYE BEER 4.8% ABV**
Hazy to the eye, this is a complex rye beer
of some originality. The rye imparts rich
spice notes.

# Iron Hill

Various locations in Delaware and Pennsylvania, **USA**
www.ironhillbrewery.com

Named after a Revolutionary War landmark in Delaware, the Iron Hill Brewery & Restaurant chain continues to grow throughout Delaware and Pennsylvania, offering a set line-up at each location but also a range of specials. Its brewers also package an Iron Hill Reserve Line in 750ml corked bottles for sale at the pubs.

### Russian Imperial Stout
IMPERIAL STOUT **9.5% ABV**
Rich, dark-chocolate aroma with supporting coffee notes. Deep chocolate flavours, balanced by roasty bitterness.

### Pig Iron Porter
PORTER **5.4% ABV**
One of their first beers. Roasted and rich, it's a full-flavoured blend of coffee, prunes, and dark cherries.

# Jacobsen Brewhouse

Gamle Carlsberg Vej 11,
DK-2500 Valby, **DENMARK**
www.jacobsenbeer.com

Named after Carlsberg's founder, Jacobsen was established in 2005 to produce high-quality speciality beers with a Scandinavian touch. This brewhouse will remain in the original 1847 Carlsberg brewery complex.

**BREWING SECRET** Jacobsen also brews an exclusive Vintage series, matured in oak barrels.

### Jacobsen Saaz Blonde
PALE ALE 7.1% ABV
Extract of angelica adds a juniper-like flavour that complements the fruity taste of the yeast.

### Jacobsen Extra Pilsner
PILSNER 5.5% ABV
A premium lager using Nordic ingredients such as Danish organic pilsner malt and Swedish sea buckthorn juice.

# Jämtlands Bryggeri

Box 224, SE-831 23 Östersund,
**SWEDEN**
www.jamtlandsbryggeri.se

This innovative small
microbrewery was established
in 1996 in the capital of the
Jämtland region of central
Sweden. It brews a wide variety
of beer, including a strong
English ale, Baltic Porter, and
Vienna lager. It consistently
wins awards at the Stockholm
Beer Festival.

**BREWING SECRETS** It draws from
British, German, and Alsace beer styles.

## President
PORTER **4.8**% ABV
This bottom-fermented beer has
a medium bitterness and the soft aroma
of Czech Saaz hops.

## Oatmeal Porter
PORTER **4.7**% ABV
An unfiltered and top-fermented porter
with a ruby-black colour. Espresso in
a glass!

# Jandelsbrunner

Hauptstr. 17, 94118 Jandelsbrunn,
**GERMANY**
www.jandelsbrunner.de

The Langs have owned this
brewery since 1810. In the 20th
century there was renewal of
equipment such as new filling
machines, and the construction
of new production plants and
maturing cellars.

**BREWING SECRET** In 2004 photovoltaic
equipment was added, to harness the
power of the sun for brewing.

## Doppelbock
**DOPPELBOCK 8% ABV**
The colour of this doppelbock is
mahogany, the taste malty, flowery, and
slightly sweet, with a nice bitter note
when finishing.

## Ur-Weizen
**WHEAT BEER 5.3% ABV**
Amber-coloured and cloudy from the
yeast, this malty beer tastes flowery
with a mild, sweet finish.

# Jennings

Cockermouth, Cumbria,
CA13 9NE **ENGLAND**
www.jenningsbrewery.co.uk

John Jennings had already been
brewing for 46 years when he
built his own brewery in 1874
in the shadow of Cockermouth
Castle. The brewery stands at the
confluence of the rivers Cocker
and Derwent, and has been
owned by Marstons since 2005.

**BREWING SECRET** Pure Lakeland water
is a key ingredient in Jennings ales.

## Cumberland Ale
BITTER 4% ABV
Florally hoppy, its intense, full flavour
and firm creamy body slide into a
dry aftertaste.

## Sneck Lifter
STRONG BITTER 5.1% ABV
Dark and fascinating, with complex
aromatics, and generous flavours of fruit
and roasted malt.

# Jever

Elisabethufer 18, 26441 Jever,
**GERMANY**
www.jever.de

Jever is one of the top breweries
in Germany. Established 160
years ago, the company started
producing its export beer in the
1950s. The pilsner as we know
it took off during the "pils-wave"
of the 1960s. Radeberger bought
Jever in 2005.

**BREWING SECRET** Jever is famous
for making one of the driest pilsners
in existence.

### Jever Fun
**LOW ALCOHOL 0.25% ABV**
Almost alcohol-free, but with a similar
taste to the pilsner. Hop-bitters and a
pilsner taste pervade this golden beer.

### Jever Pilsener
**PILSNER 4.8% ABV**
The master brewers use a lot of hops at
Jever, and their bitterness makes this
pilsner very dry.

# Jolly Pumpkin

3115 Broad Street, Dexter,
Michigan 48130, **USA**
www.jollypumpkin.com

Not quite like any other brewery
in the USA, Jolly Pumpkin
Artisan Ales allows its beers to
develop under the influence of
local wild yeast. All beers are
aged in barrels, and are often
blended and re-fermentated in
the bottle to deliver effervescent
beer. Though its output is small,
the brewery has developed a
national following.

## Oro de Calabaza
BELGIAN STRONG GOLDEN ALE 8% ABV
Golden and cloudy, tart and spicy,
with orchard fruit and citrus. Develops
with age.

## Bam Biere
SAISON 4.5% ABV
The whole exceeds the sum of its parts
in this "farmhouse" ale, from the hops
(billowing head, dry finish) to the
spicy malts.

# Jopen

Minckelersweg 2a,
2031 EM Haarlem, **NETHERLANDS**
www.jopen.nl

Jopen was founded in 1995 with the intention of recreating old beer styles specifically from the Haarlem locale – once an important brewing centre. This is Holland's only brewery to concentrate on local recipes, and no other in the world produces beer in these styles. A brewpub to showcase the beers is due to open soon.

### Jopen Koyt
GRUIT BEER **8.5%** ABV

A recreation of a pre-hop beer brewed from three grains and herbs. Fruity, spicy, and delicious.

### Jopen Hoppenbier
AMBER ALE **6.5%** ABV

Based on a recipe from 1501 using barley, wheat, and oats; hints of coriander, ginger, and cloves complement spicy hops.

# Kelham Island

Sheffield, South Yorkshire,
S3 8SA **ENGLAND**
www.kelhambrewery.co.uk

Since Kelham Island opened in 1990, Sheffield's four large breweries have closed down, which makes Kelham's success all the more remarkable. An astonishing range of awards has been collected along the way.

**BREWING SECRET** Pale Rider and Easy Rider both make great use of highly fragrant American hops.

### Pale Rider
STRONG BITTER 5.2% ABV
Strong but delicately fruity multi-award winner, which profits from an adventurous use of American hops.

### Easy Rider
BITTER 4.3% ABV
A subtle pale ale, its initial crisp bitterness surrendering only to a lingering fruity palate.

# Keo

Franklin Roosevelt Ave, Limassol,
3602 **CYPRUS**
www.keogroup.com

Limassol is the main port and
fastest-growing city on the island
of Cyprus. It is also home to the
Keo Brewery, and no trip to
Limassol is complete without
visiting the plant, which lies just
beyond the Old Port. During
the week there is a daily tour
around the brewery – finishing,
of course, in the tasting room.

## Keo
LAGER 4.5% ABV
A pale lager with a thick head and
a sweet malt taste, it is easy on the
palate and very drinkable.

## Five Beer
LAGER 5% ABV
Deep amber in colour, it is rich in malt
and low in bitterness. Sweet in the finish.

# Klein Duimpje

Parallelweg 2, 2182 CP Hillegom,
**NETHERLANDS**
www.kleinduimpje.nl

This is the brewery of a prize-winning amateur brewer, Erik Bouman, whose porter was chosen as the best of more than 400 entries at the Dutch Homebrewing Championship of 1997. Bouman's competition success prompted him to start brewing professionally. His extensive range of top-fermenting ales includes his celebrated porter.

### Hillegoms Tarwe Bier
**WITBIER 5.5% ABV**
Flavoured with coriander and orange peel, this wheat beer is spicy, citric, and just ever so slightly sweet.

### Porter
**PORTER 5.5% ABV**
Espresso-like roast malt combines with a chocolate sweetness, backed up with liquorice and toast.

# Kona

75-5629 Kuakini Highway, Kailua
Kona, Hawaii 97640, **USA**
www.konabrewingco.com

Sales are booming everywhere
for Kona Brewing, which offers
mainland drinkers "a pint of
paradise". The Big Island
brewery added capacity to meet
growing demand in Hawaii,
while sales in 17 mainland states
have increased even faster. Beers
sold on the mainland are made
under contract at Widmer
Brothers in Oregon.

### Pipeline Porter
PORTER **5.4%** ABV
Brewed with local Kona coffee, its flavour
is well-integrated. Roasty malt, oily, with
chocolate notes.

### Fire Rock Pale Ale
PALE ALE **6%** ABV
Reddish orange with slightly sweet
caramel aromas and flavour, spicy
and citric hops are cleverly integrated
and balanced.

# König Ludwig

Augsburger Stre. 41, 82256
Fürstenfeldbruck, **GERMANY**
www.kaltenberg.de

The history of the Bavarian royal
family, the Wittelsbachers, is
closely connected with the art
of beer-making. Today, HRH
Luitpold Prince of Bavaria
continues the family business
successfully with his brands
König Ludwig and Kaltenberg.
The latter brand name refers to
the brewery at Kaltenberg Castle.

### König Ludwig Dunkel

DUNKEL 5.1% ABV

Amber, with a smooth taste of dark malt
and fine hops, this is the most popular
dunkel in Germany.

### König Ludwig Weissbier

WHEAT BEER 5.5% ABV

One of the most popular wheat beers in
Bavaria; cloudy yellow, with fine hops
in the finish. A very traditional, non-
filtered speciality.

# De Koninck

Mechelse Steenweg 291,
B2018 Antwerpen, **BELGIUM**
www.dekoninck.be

De Koninck is an icon – as is its
main beer. It embodies the town
of Antwerp – whose inhabitants
are a proud lot, and will say so.
The amber "bolleke" (actually the
glass) is still the staple diet in
many bars.

**BREWING SECRET** The draught version
is unpasteurized and should ideally be
tasted at its source.

### De Koninck

AMBER "SPECIALE BELGE" 5% ABV
Amber malts, residual sugars, and hops
give excellent balance to a fine ale, with
a slight but distinct sulphury aroma and
biscuit character. The draught version
is particularly good – available in cask
in the UK as well.

# Krone Tettnang

Bärenplatz 7, 88069 Tettnang,
**GERMANY**
www.krone-tettnang.de

Krone Tettnang is a small craft
brewery that has been owned by
the Tauscher family for seven
generations. It is a member of
"Brewers with Body and Soul" –
a group of ten small companies
who aim to produce beer "in
another, but traditional, way...".

**BREWING SECRET** The first organic
beer of the Bodensee region was made
here in 1993.

## Keller-Pils

PILSNER 4.7% ABV
The famous first organic beer of the
region. Unfiltered and cloudy, it has the
typical pilsner bitterness of hops and
some sweetness of malt.

## Kronenbier

LAGER 4.9% ABV
Richly flavoured traditional beer with the
finest possible malt aroma, and a light
finish of fine hops.

# Krušovice

270 53 Krušovice 1,
**CZECH REPUBLIC**
www.pivo-krusovice.cz

When the original owner, Jiří Birka, offered the brewery for sale in 1581 to Emperor Rudolf II, the inventory read: "The brewery kettle is made of stone, so it may be cooked upon immediately". Those documents still exist, but Birka would hardly recognize the highly-mechanized, industrial brewery today – currently the nation's fifth-largest producer.

### Krušovice Imperial
**PREMIUM LAGER 5.5% ABV**
A dry straw aroma heightens a bitter palate, with a floral hop and malt finish.

### Krušovice Dark Beer
**DARK BEER 3.8% ABV**
Roast malt and caramel generosity meet earthy and nutty nuances before a citrus hop finale.

# Kuhnhenn

5919 Chicago Road, Warren,
Michigan 48092, **USA**
www.kbrewery.com

Brothers Brett and Eric
Kuhnhenn turned the hardware
store their father ran for 35 years
into a small brewery, winery,
meadery, and brew-on-premises
(where customers can make their
own beer). The national
reputation of Kuhnhenn shows
how word of mouth – and the
Internet – can help small
breweries develop a cult following.

### Raspberry Eisbock
EISBOCK **10.6**% ABV
A small-run beer. Complex, rich with
raspberries, chocolate, warming alcohol,
and a closing tartness.

### Penetration Porter
PORTER **5.9**% ABV
Almost black, with roasted coffee,
chocolate, and dark fruits like cherry
filling the nose and the mouth. Citrusy
hop finish.

# Kulmbacher

Lichtenfelser Str. 9, 95326
Kulmbach, **GERMANY**
www.kulmbacher.de

The name of Kulmbach, a city
in northern Bavaria, is known
to beer-lovers throughout the
world. Its fame began with
the offerings of beer master
Wolfgang Reichel in 1846. Since
his time, many other brands
have joined the company, and
production is now about 300
million litres (70 million gallons)
of beer each year.

### Mönchshof Schwarzbier
SCHWARZBIER **4.9**% ABV
Dark roasted malts and fine hops. The
deep, dark colour and fine aroma are
typical of schwarzbiers.

### Kapuziner Weissbier
WHEAT BEER **5.4**% ABV
Naturally cloudy, sparkling and with
a sweet and fruity taste; this unfiltered
beer is typical of the wheat beer style.

# Lagunitas

1280 North McDowell Boulevard,
Petaluma, California 94954, **USA**
www.lagunitas.com

Always known for its hop-driven
beers, Lagunitas launched a
new range in 2006, each one
commemorating a Frank Zappa
album and released 40 years
after the album of the same
name. Founder Tony Magee
obtained the permission of the
Zappa Family Trust to use the
original album art on the bottle
label for these beers.

### India Pale Ale
INDIA PALE ALE 5.7% ABV
Brimming with hop character – orange,
grapefruit, peaches, pine – over
malty sweetness.

### Kill Ugly Radio
INDIA PALE ALE 7.8% ABV
Only in the USA is this an IPA.
Caramel and fermentation fruit are
balanced by spicy, citrusy, and bitter
Northwest hops.

# Lakefront

1872 North Commerce Street,
Milwaukee, Wisconsin 53212, **USA**
www.lakefrontbrewery.com

Lakefront Brewing, known since
1987 for a range of robust beers,
recently moved to the fore in
brewing New Grist gluten-free
beer for coeliacs who cannot
tolerate the grains traditionally
used in making beer.

**BREWING SECRET** New Grist is brewed
from sorghum, hops, water, rice, and
gluten-free yeast grown on molasses.

## New Grist

**GLUTEN FREE 5% ABV**
A tang of citrus zest to start, then
a light palate with hints of fruit. Mildy
astringent and tart.

## Riverwest Stein

**VIENNA LAGER 6% ABV**
Lightly toasted aromas with hints
of caramel. More caramel in the
mouth, and hop citrus fruitiness.
Woody undertones.

# Lambrate

Via Adelchi 5, 20131 Milano, **ITALY**
www.birrificiolambrate.com

The first (and still the best) brewpub in Milan, founded in 1996 by brothers Davide and Giampaolo Sangiorgi and their friend Fabio Brocca after a visit to 't IJ Brewery in Amsterdam. They have recently expanded production, adding some interesting new ales. The menu features some creative beer-influenced dishes, such as pork cooked in beer mash.

### Ghisa

SMOKED ALE 5% ABV

Ebony in colour with a "cappuccino" foam; lighty smoked, easy to drink, and balanced, with plum notes and a long, hoppy finish.

### Montestella

BLOND ALE 4.9% ABV

Their flagship ale; pale, with fresh aromas of hay and hops with a long, dry finish cleansing the palate.

# Lao Brewery

Km 12 Thadeua Road,
Vientiane, **LAOS**
www.beer-lao.com

The Lao Brewery began
production in 1973 and was
originally known as Brasseries
et Glaci è res du Laos. Two years
later, in 1975, it became state
owned. In 2002, Carlsberg and
TCC, a Thai company, each
agreed to acquire a 25 per cent
stake in Lao Brewery; the
remaining shares are still held
by the Laos government.

### Beerlao
LAGER **5**% ABV
Described as Asia's best beer, Beerlao has
a pleasant sweetness. Light bitterness,
with hints of honey.

### Beerlao Dark
LAGER **6.5**% ABV
Reddish brown, it is full of sweet
toffee and toast flavours. A short but
warming finish.

# Lees

Manchester, M24 2AX **ENGLAND**
www.jwlees.co.uk

Established by the far-sighted John Lees in 1878, when Manchester was becoming the "workshop of the world", Lees expanded rapidly, matching the growing local thirst. Sixth-generation family members currently run the brewery and pub estate, and they remain faithful to the brewery's maxim: "We think of ourselves as old-fashioned and cutting-edge".

## Moonraker

BARLEY WINE 7.5% ABV
Powerfully fruity on a rich roast malt base, with a sweet tendency and dryish finish.

## JW Lees Bitter

BITTER 4% ABV
Classic amber-coloured northern bitter, with layers of malt in the mouthfeel and a citrus finale.

# Lefebvre

54, Rue du Croly,
B1430 Quenast, **BELGIUM**
www.brasserielefebvre.be

The first member of the Lefebvre family to be involved in brewing was Jules in 1876. The brewery is now in the hands of the sixth generation, with Paul Lefebvre.

**BREWING SECRET** For a family brewery, this one is very outward looking, and now 80 per cent of its beer production is exported.

### Floreffe Double
BROWN ABBEY ALE **6.3**% ABV
An ale of a chocolatey kind, which develops madeira and port notes with a little ageing.

### Saison 1900
SAISON **5.2**% ABV
One of the few that refers to the brewery's past; delicate farmyard and rose water aromas.

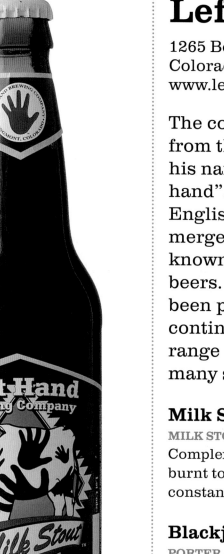

# Left Hand

1265 Boston Avenue, Longmont, Colorado 80501, **USA**
www.lefthandbrewing.com

The company takes its name from the Arapahoe Chief Niwot, his name translating as "left hand". Originally brewing English-style ales, the brewery merged in 1998 with Tabernash, known for Bavarian-inspired beers. Those beers have now been phased out, but Left Hand continues to develop a wide range of beer styles and produces many seasonal brews too.

### Milk Stout
MILK STOUT 5.3% ABV
Complex and smooth, chocolate and burnt toast in the aroma and flavour constantly balanced by creamy sweetness.

### Blackjack Porter
PORTER 5.2% ABV
Chocolate and liquorice aromas, medium body, with hints of dark cherries and a smooth, dry finish.

# Leinenkugel's

1 Jefferson Avenue, Chippewa Falls,
Wisconsin 54729, **USA**
www.leinie.com

Since 1988, when Miller Brewing
bought a controlling interest, the
Jacob Leinenkugel Brewing
Company has grown into one
of the largest regional breweries
in the country, distributing in
almost every state.

**BREWING SECRET** The brewery,
founded in 1867, still offers a range
reflecting its German heritage.

### Creamy Dark
US DARK LAGER **4.9**% ABV
As creamy as promised, chocolate with
coffee and cream character and a dryish
not-too-bitter finish.

### Sunset Wheat
US WHEAT BEER **4.9**% ABV
Light but complex beer, almost a fruit
salad of aromas and flavours, with some
wheaty tartness and coriander spiciness.

# Liefmans

Aalststraat 200,
B9700 Oudenaarde, **BELGIUM**
www.liefmans.be

Although Liefmans parent group went into receivership at the end 2007, it looks likely that Duvel Moortgat will take over, and so the Oudenaarde plant has a good chance of survival – if, as before, for lagering purposes only.

**BREWING SECRET** Liefmans beers are rare survivors from the once famous Oudenaards bruin style.

## Liefmans Goudenband
OUD BRUIN **8%** ABV
A strong interpretation of the style, its underlying acidity lending the beer outstanding ageing possibilities.

## Liefmans Kriek
OUD BRUIN **6%** ABV
The lighter version, refermented with sour cherries. The rare, unsweetened draught version is stellar.

# Lindemans

Lenniksebaan 1479, B1602
Vlezenbeek, **BELGIUM**
www.lindemans.be

When considering lambic breweries, we tend to think about small farm brewers. Lindemans may seem to fit this bill at first glance, yet it is also on the margins of the 10 largest breweries in Belgium. Its success is owed to the rather sweetish fruit concoctions it excels in, with nearly half of the produce destined for foreign markets.

### Lindemans Gueuze Cuvée René

GUEUZE 5% ABV
Initially produced on demand for export, now this caramel-and-sour-apple gueuze is fairly common.

### Lindemans Kriek Cuvée René

KRIEK 5% ABV
Unfiltered kriek is rare and this bottled beer is a dry notch above the draught sweet version.

# Lion

700 North Pennsylvania Avenue,
Wilkes-Barre, Pennsylvania 18705,
**USA**
www.lionbrewery.com

The Lion Brewery, founded in
1905, is a survivor – the last of
dozens of breweries that once
operated in northeastern
Pennsylvania. Most recently
the brewery has emphasized
this heritage with its Stegmaier
brand of good-value traditional
beers, the roots of which go back
to 1857.

### Steg 150
VIENNA LAGER 5.5% ABV
Created to celebrate the brewery's 150th
anniversary. Smells like warm toast,
malt-accented, lightly sweet but smooth,
not cloying.

### Stegmaier Porter
PORTER 5.5% ABV
Notes of sweet chocolate and ripe fruit
matched with toasty malt and a coffee-
bitter finish.

# Lion Brewery

254 Colombo Road, Biyagama,
**SRI LANKA**
www.lionbeer.com

The company's best-known beer
is the bottle conditioned Lion
Stout. The beer is brewed from
British, Czech, and Danish
malts, with Styrian hops and
an English yeast strain. All the
ingredients are transported
along precarious roads to
the brewery, located 3,500ft
(1,000m) above sea level in
the midst of tea plantations.

### Lion Stout
STOUT 8% ABV
A world-class beer, with pruney, mocha
aromas and flavours. It has a tar-like
oiliness of body and a peppery, bitter-
chocolate finish. The alcohol gives it
a long warming finish.

# Little Creatures

40 Mews Road, Fremantle,
Western Australia 6160,
**AUSTRALIA**
www.littlecreatures.com.au

Based in an enormous hangar-like building on the water's edge at Fremantle, Little Creatures combines a bar/restaurant within a busy microbrewery. The flagship Pale Ale is inspired by the likes of the US-based Sierra Nevada, and, along with the venue, has been a runaway success. The company is currently gearing up production, and has announced bold plans for themed bars in Sydney and Melbourne, and a second brewery to be built in Victoria.

### Little Creatures Pale Ale
US PALE ALE **5.2%** ABV
Citrus/grapefruit hop aromatics; chewy malt and citrus-tinged, robust bitterness.

### Rogers' Beer
AMBER ALE **3.8%** ABV
Biscuity malt notes; caramel-laced mid-palate and spicy-citrus hoppiness; short finish.

# Locher

Industriestrasse 12, CH - 9050
Appenzell, **SWITZERLAND**
www.appenzellerbier.ch

Appenzell is Switzerland's
smallest province (kanton), but
the beer produced by the local
brewery has won it a lot of fame.

**BREWING SECRET** In the 1990s, the
Locher family found out that beers
brewed on the full moon ferment more
easily; they have, therefore, created a line
of "Vollmond-brews".

### Vollmond

ORGANIC LAGER **5.2%** ABV
An aroma of hops and lemon zest;
medium body – chewy; hoppy, but
not excessively bitter.

### Holzfass-Bier

LAGER **5.2%** ABV
Aromas of sweetcorn, very little
carbonation, and a distinctive note
from the oak in which it is matured.

# Lord Nelson

19 Kent Street, The Rocks, Sydney,
New South Wales 2000, **AUSTRALIA**
www.lordnelsonbrewery.com

Still going strong after 20-plus years, Sydney's original modern brewpub attracts ale lovers to this historic hotel, which claims to be the city's "oldest continuously licensed pub". The early brews were basic malt extract-based beers, but have evolved into tasty and complex ales, worthy of this gem of a watering hole.

### Old Admiral
STRONG ALE **6.1%** ABV
Dense, malty palate, with plummy notes, lively bitterness, and a warming afterglow.

### Three Sheets
PALE ALE **4.9%** ABV
Malty, fruity aromatics; malt-accented, with citrus and apricot hints; well-rounded bitterness.

# Lost Abbey

155 Mata Way, San Marcos,
California 92069, **USA**
www.lostabbey.com

Port Brewing, born out of a chain
of brewpubs, launched the Lost
Abbey brand in 2006, and quickly
built up a devoted following.
Brewmaster Tomme Arthur
oversees the ageing room,
conjuring up what are best
thought of as "Wild American"
ales – malt-accented beers
enhanced by the barrels in
which they are matured.

**BREWING SECRET** The wooden barrels
that once held wines and whiskies now
nurture wild yeasts.

## Red Poppy
SOUR ALE **5.5**% ABV
Brown ale with sour cherries, aged in
French oak wine barrels for a year.
Oaky, with pleasing acidity.

## Judgment Day
BELGIAN STRONG DARK ALE **10.5**% ABV
Dark and powerful, with profoundly fruity
aromas and palate; chocolate and whisky
malt undertones.

The Lost Abbey

Red Poppy Ale
MALT BEVERAGE BREWED WITH CHERRIES
ALC. 5% BY VOL. AGED IN OAK BARRELS 12.7 OUNCES
Brewed and Bottled by Port Brewing Company, San Marcos CA

# Löwenbräu

Nymphenburger Str. 7, 80335
München, **GERMANY**
www.loewenbraeu.de

Löwenbräu is one of the most
famous brands in the world. The
company is more than 500 years
old. In 1948, only three years
after the end of World War II,
Löwenbräu began exporting
again: first to Switzerland, then
further afield. In 1997 there was a
marriage between Löwenbräu
and Spatenbräu; today both are
part of the global player InBev.

### Löwenbräu Triumphator
DOPPELBOCK 7.6% ABV
Dark brown in colour, the Triumphator
has a strong flavour of malt, but only
a subtle aroma of hops. Sweet.

### Löwenbräu Urtyp
EXPORT 5.4% ABV
A balanced flavour with fine aromas of
malt; full-bodied, pleasant, and fresh, with
mild hops in the finish.

# Mad River

195 Taylor Way, Blue Lake,
California 95525, **USA**
www.madriverbrewing.com

Founder Bob Smith built his
brewery in 1989 using recycled
materials, and has since received
many awards for its waste-
reduction programmes. Mad
River reuses 98 per cent of its
residuals and generates just
one cubic metre/yard of waste
a month while brewing about
250,000 gallons of beer per year.

### Jamaica Red Ale

AMBER ALE **6.6**% ABV
First made for the annual reggae festival.
Sweetish nose, with Crystal malts and
solid, refreshing hops.

### Steelhead Scotch Porter

PORTER **6.4**% ABV
Distinctly a porter, with roasted malt and
a touch of sourness. Caramel notes and
hints of smoke add complexity.

# Magic Hat

5 Bartlett Road, Burlington,
Vermont 05403, **USA**
www.magichat.net

Magic Hat's unique and sometimes outrageous packaging and its "non-style" beers have brought double-digit growth year after year. It began in 2008 with construction underway to double capacity, and plans to push distribution into the midwest and south.

**BREWING SECRET** The Orlio range of beers are certified organic.

### #9
PALE ALE **4.6**% ABV
Apricot-infused. Subtle stone fruits on the palate, sometimes buttery notes. Finishes dry.

### Roxy Rolles
AMBER ALE **5.8**% ABV
Brewed for the winter season, rich with caramel and grapefruit aromas and flavours, balanced by closing bitterness.

# Maisel

Hindenburgstr. 9, 95445 Bayreuth,
**GERMANY**
www.maisel.com

Hans and Eberhardt Maisel founded the brewery in the city of Richard Wagner in 1887. The family decided to concentrate the production on wheat beer in 1955, and Maisel became a trendsetter for this style.

**BREWING SECRET** Their success is the result of a high level of ability in the hand-crafting of beers.

## Maisel's Weisse

WHEAT BEER 5.2% ABV
The colour is typical for Maisel: a gleaming red. Fermentation in the bottle gives the beer fruity notes and mild nuttiness in the finish.

## Maisel's Dampfbier

SPECIAL BEER 4.9% ABV
A very old-fashioned beer: the mix of different malts gives it a really special, fine character.

# Malt Shovel

99 Pyrmont Bridge Road,
Camperdown, Sydney,
New South Wales 2050, **AUSTRALIA**
www.maltshovel.com.au

Positioned as Lion Nathan's craft brewing arm, the Malt Shovel Brewery has an impressive portfolio of beer styles under brewmaster Dr Charles "Chuck" Hahn. The brewery's first release in 1998 was Amber Ale, which found ready acceptance with traditional lager drinkers. Their James Squire brands are named after a former convict and highwayman, who became the colony's first successful hop grower and brewer.

### Malt Shovel India Pale Ale
INDIA PALE ALE 5.6% ABV
Chewy, caramel-tinged maltiness balanced by robust (dry-hopped) hop flavour and lingering bitterness.

### James Squire Porter
PORTER 5% ABV
Hints of coffee, dark chocolate, and dark fruit (plums); a sumptuous beer, with a smooth finish.

# Marston's

Burton upon Trent, Staffordshire,
DE14 2BW **ENGLAND**
www.marstonsbeercompany.co.uk

The company operates three
sites: the Park Brewery in
Wolverhampton, which brews
Banks's, Hanson's, and Mansfield
beers; Jennings Brewery at
Cockermouth in the Lake
District, and the Albion Brewery
in Burton upon Trent.
Throughout its long existence
it has acquired several of its
competitors. Then, in 1999,
Marston's itself was taken over
by Wolverhampton & Dudley
Breweries, which changed its
name to Marston's PLC in 2007.

### Pedigree
BEST BITTER 4.4% ABV
A British institution – sweetly hop-laden,
with the vague sulphur aroma that's
characteristic of Burton ales.

### Old Empire
INDIA PALE ALE 5.7% ABV
A stylish India Pale Ale, with hop and
fruit flavours and a dry extra-hop finish.

# Matilda Bay

130 Stirling Highway, North
Fremantle, Western Australia 6159,
**AUSTRALIA**
www.matildabay.com.au

Australia's first modern craft
brewery kicked off in Fremantle
in 1984, was acquired by
Foster's six years later, and
has been revitalized in recent
times. Original brews such as
Redback (a hefeweizen) and
Dogbolter (a dark lager) have
been supplemented with a wide
range of beer styles. Much of
the new direction occurred
under the watch of head brewer
Brad Rogers, who has since
left the Foster's fold to embark
on a new brewing venture.

### Dogbolter
DARK LAGER 5.2% ABV
Roasty, dark chocolate notes; complex
mid-palate; smooth, coffee-ish finish.

### Bohemian Pilsner
CZECH PILSNER 5% ABV
A solid maltiness to the pilsner
is well balanced with a generous
hop bitterness.

# McAuslan

5080 St-Ambroise, Montréal,
Québec, H4C 2G1, **CANADA**
www.mcauslan.com

McAuslan Brewing began
in January of 1989 when its
founder Peter McAuslan decided
to turn his home-brewing
hobby into a business. It quickly
established itself as one of the
area's best microbreweries
and was one of the first in
Canada to bottle its products.
It produces a challenging range
of seasonal beers.

### St-Ambroise Apricot Ale

FRUITY WHEAT BEER 5% ABV

Apricot essence and malted wheat
combine to create an original tasting
beer with a clean, fruit nose.

### St-Ambroise Oatmeal Stout

STOUT 5% ABV

Brewed from dark malts and roasted
barley, this stout carries strong espresso
and chocolate notes.

# Meantime

Greenwich, London, SE7 8RX
**ENGLAND**
www.meantimebrewing.com

Preferring to be known as the brewery that can't be pigeonholed could be self-regarding, but the approach of master brewer Alastair Hook is purposeful – to demonstrate the exciting flavour potential that beer has to offer.

**BREWING SECRET** Research into, and recreation of, beers from the past is an abiding passion here, as exemplified by Meantime's India Pale Ale.

## Meantime Chocolate

SPECIALITY STRONG BEER **6.5**% ABV
Complex malt structure, with dark chocolate releasing vanilla notes to create a rich, memorable infusion.

## India Pale Ale

INDIA PALE ALE **7.5**% ABV
Massively hoppy, with herbal, spice, and grass tiers grasping the strength of the original IPAs.

# Mendocino

South Highway 101, Hopland,
California 13351, **USA**
www.mendobrew.com

Mendocino Brewing was one of
the first success stories among
US "boutique" breweries (as
they were called at the time).
It opened in 1983 as the Hopland
Brewery, having acquired
equipment, the house yeast, and
even a few employees from the
groundbreaking, but by then
defunct, New Albion Brewery.

### Red Tail Ale

AMBER ALE **6.1%** ABV
An earthy nose includes hints of orchard
fruits. Layers of creamy malt with notes
of liquorice.

### Blue Heron

PALE ALE **6.1%** ABV
Orange zest and lemon rind to start,
giving way to traditional biscuity malt
and a balanced, moderate bitterness.

# Mettlacher Abteibräu

Bahnhofstr. 32, 66693 Mettlach,
**GERMANY**
www.abtei-brauerei.de

Mettlacher specializes in natural,
unfiltered beer. Guests can
watch the brewing process from
the attached restaurant. The
brewers promote the beer styles
of the region and run courses
on beer production.

**BREWING SECRET** High-quality basic
products, modern techniques, and the
energy of the brewers ensure success.

### Abtei-Bock
BOCK 6.2% ABV
Strong-roasted bock with obvious roasty
aromas and an even more intense flavour
of fine hops.

### Abtei-Josef-Sud
WHEAT BEER 5.1% ABV
The dark amber-coloured wheat beer is
sparkling and has typical aromas from
the mash of wheat and barley malts.

2

# Michigan

1093 Highview Drive, Webberville,
Michigan 48892, **USA**
www.michiganbrewing.com

Although Michigan Brewing
was one of the state's biggest
breweries before it bought
the defunct Celis brand from
international giant Miller, it is
now best known for that range
of beers. Belgian in style, they
were first created by Pierre
Celis (brewer of the original
Hoegaarden beer) after he
moved to Texas. Celis even
helped brew the first batches
made in Michigan.

## Celis White
WITBIER 4.25% ABV
Cloudy, coriander-spicy, with citrus all
the way through, wheat tartness, and
a soft finish.

## Mackinac Pale Ale
PALE ALE 5.5% ABV
The brewery flagship, golden-orange,
not quite pale, with substantial malt
fruitiness. Earthy and citrusy
American hops.

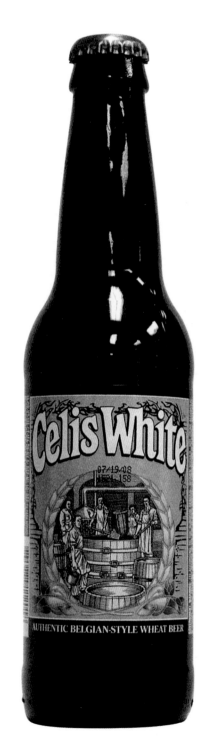

# Mikkeller

Slien 2, 2.tv,
DK-1766 Copenhagen, **DENMARK**
www.mikkeller.dk

An innovative brewery producing an eclectic range of beer. Mikkeller adopts an American rule-breaking approach to brewing and has achieved significant international recognition with several of its brews.

**BREWING SECRET** The brewery recently introduced Black, the strongest beer ever made by a Danish brewer.

### Beer Geek Breakfast
OATMEAL STOUT **7.5% ABV**
An award-winning stout with a rich nose, smooth and balanced taste, and coffee and chocolate notes.

### Black
IMPERIAL STOUT **17.5% ABV**
Exceptional body of sugars, roasted coffee beans, and black chocolate; a complex and lingering aftertaste.

# Minhas

1208 14th Avenue, Monroe,
Wisconsin 53566, **USA**
www.minhasbrewery.com

Ravinder Minhas was just 24
years old when he bought the
historic Joseph Huber Brewery
in 2006 to produce his popular
Mountain Creek brands, already
brewed under contract in Monroe
for Canadian distribution.
Minhas Craft Brewery still makes
the Huber brands (dating back to
1843), Berghoff beers, and a line
of grocery store house label
beers as well.

### Lazy Mutt
GOLDEN ALE **4.8**% ABV
The first released under the Minhas
brand, billed as a "farmhouse ale" by
the brewery but more summer ale than
a *saison*.

### Huber Bock
BOCK **5.4**% ABV
Toasty and dry, with caramel notes. Best
at Baumgartner's Cheese Store & Tavern
near the brewery.

# Minoh AJI

3-19-11 Makiochi, Minoh City,
Osaka 562-0004, **JAPAN**
www.minoh-beer.jp

Established by liquor store
owner Masaji Oshita, and run by
his daughters Kaori and Mayuko,
Minoh AJI brewery mostly makes
beers based on American craft
beer styles.

**BREWING SECRET** Among the more
individual beers are two that contain
hemp and one that uses Cabernet
Sauvignon grape juice.

## Minoh AJI Stout
STOUT 5.5% ABV
Brewed in the Irish style, with lots of
roast flavour and creamy texture, this
stout has a subdued bitterness.

## Double IPA
STRONG IPA 9% ABV
Bold and exciting, this strong beer is
only produced as a seasonal so far, but
its popularity may lead to it becoming
available year-round.

# Moa

Jacksons Rd, RD3 Blenheim,
**NEW ZEALAND**
www.moabeer.co.nz

Nestled among vines in
Marlborough's wine country
is Moa's brewery and tasting
room – the brainchild of
winemaker Josh Scott, who
wanted to make super premium
beers with the winemaking
techniques used for Champagne-
style sparkling wines.

**BREWING SECRET** Moa's larger
750ml bottles undergo the full *méthode
traditionelle* production regime.

## Moa Original

BOTTLE-CONDITIONED PILS 5.5% ABV
Extended yeast contact rewards this
delightful dry, crisp pilsner with
a savoury toastiness.

## Moa Blanc

BOTTLE-CONDITIONED
WHEAT BEER 5.5% ABV
Dry, crisp, hints of banana and
vanilla; soft natural carbonation.

# Moctezuma

Monterrey/Veracruz-Llave, **MEXICO**
www.femsa.com

Mexico's most innovative brewer, Moctezuma also has operations in Brazil and is an important exporter of beer to the USA. It has a powerful brand portfolio that includes Tecate, Dos Equis, Sol, Indio, Bohemia, and Carta Blanc, many of which are sold in style bars worldwide. Its beers tend to be smooth, with a spritzy finish.

### Dos Equis
**VIENNA LAGER 4.8% ABV**
Rich and dark red, with chocolate orange flavours; its warming sweetness gives way to a long finish.

### Sol
**LAGER 4.5% ABV**
A crisp, light-bodied lager with a corn syrup aroma.

# De Molen

Overtocht 43, 2411 BS Bodegraven,
**NETHERLANDS**
www.brouwerijdemolen.nl

Since starting Molen in 2004,
brewer Menno Olivier has
quickly gained an enviable
reputation. This is one of only
a handful of Dutch micros to
export; its cask-conditioned beer,
Engel, is designed especially for
the UK market.

**BREWING SECRET** Aficionados regard
Tsarina Esra, an Imperial porter, as one
of Europe's very finest beers.

## Borefts Blond

BLOND ALE 6.5% ABV
Unlike many blonds, hops dominate here.
Orange, pine, resin, and grass flavours fill
the mouth.

## Borefts Stout

STOUT 7% ABV
Packed with all the roasty malt flavours
you expect from a stout. Complex,
characterful, harmonious.

# Biervision Monstein

Monstein, CH-7278 Davos,
**SWITZERLAND**
www.biervision-monstein.ch

Andreas Aegerter and Christian
Ochs started this village brewery
high up in the mountains near
Davos in 2001, together with 756
small investors (each of them a
devoted customer). They all
shared the vision that there is a
market for unusual beers, as well
as beer-related products, such as
cheese crusted with malt and
spirits distilled from beer.

### Mungga
KÖLSCH **3.5%** ABV
Brewed from organic Swiss ingredients,
Mungga ("groundhog") has aromas
of violets, a dry taste, and an
elegant bitterness.

### Royal 11
SPICED BEER **6.5%** ABV
Reddish, with pleasant cherry aromas
(from the local liqueur Röteli); fruity
and only faintly bitter.

# Moo Brew

655 Main Road, Berriedale, Hobart,
Tasmania 7011, **AUSTRALIA**
www.moobrew.com.au

A stunningly appointed
microbrewery, with commanding
views of Derwent River and
Mount Wellington from the
second-storey, glass-fronted
brewhouse. An off-shoot of
Moorilla Estate winery, Moo
Brew has set a new benchmark
among Australian craft
producers, with slick packaging,
uncompromising beers, and
premium pricing.

## Moo Brew Pilsner

CZECH PILSNER 5% ABV
Bright, golden, with finely-beaded
bubbles; honey-ish malt character
balanced by herbal hop bitterness.

## Moo Brew Pale Ale

US PALE ALE 4.9% ABV
Citrus aromatics; grapefruit notes
dominate mid-palate, rounded out with
substantial, tingling bitter finish.

# Moorhouse's

Burnley, Lancashire, BB11 5EN
**ENGLAND**
www.moorhouses.co.uk

Mineral water and low-alcohol
"hop bitters" were William
Moorhouse's forte. He started
his business in 1865, but his
successors failed to achieve a
great deal in terms of brewing
beer until fresh investment in
infrastructure arrived in 1988.
Further improvements and
additions accelerated growth
and helped create the admirable
reputation that Moorhouse
ales have today.

### Pendle Witches Brew
STRONG BITTER 5.1% ABV
Distinctive and amber-coloured, the beer
has a full malty palate and a resonant
fruity hop finale.

### Black Cat
MILD 3.4% ABV
Full, dark, and complex, with distinctive
chocolate malt and liquorice flavours,
and a hoppy finish.

# Moosehead

89 Main Street West, Saint John,
New Brunswick, E2M 3H2, **CANADA**
www.moosehead.ca

Canada's oldest independent
brewery can trace its roots back
to 1867, when Susannah Oland
first started brewing in her
Dartmouth, Nova Scotia
backyard. Today, the company
is still owned and operated by
the Oland family. Moosehead
has stakes in McAuslan and
wholly owns the Niagara Falls
Brewing Company.

### Moosehead Lager
LAGER 5% ABV
Pale straw-coloured, clean-tasting
session beer, best drunk cold.

### Clancy Amber Ale
ALE 5% ABV
Top-fermented, Clancy's is a reddish beer,
with a distinct malt aroma and overlays of
caramel.

# Multi Bintang

Surabaya, Central Java, **INDONESIA**
www.multibintang.co.id

Indonesia's largest brewery produces and markets a range of drinks, including Bir Bintang, Heineken, Guinness Stout, and the low alcohol Green Sands. It was founded in 1929, with Heineken taking a share of the company in the 1930s. Though taken over by the Indonesian government in 1957, Heineken became involved again in 1967, and today it is largely owned by them.

### Bintang Bir Pilsener
LAGER 4.8% ABV
A fresh malty aroma gives way to a dry hoppy bitter finish – the beer clearly draws on its Dutch ancestry.

### Bintang Gold
LAGER 4.8% ABV
A slightly darker variation of the pilsener, brewed to commemorate the republic's golden anniversary.

# New Belgium

500 Linden Street, Fort Collins,
Colorado 80524, **USA**
www.newbelgium.com

Jeff Lebesch and Kim Jordan
started out with a system, built
to Belgian specifications, in their
cellar in 1991. They now operate
the third largest craft brewery
in the USA. Best known for Fat
Tire Ale, the brewery offers
quite a wide range of beers,
including its outstanding Blue
Paddle Pilsener.

**BREWING SECRET** New Belgium has
more capacity for ageing beer on wood
than any brewery other than Rodenbach
Brewery in Belgium.

## Fat Tire

AMBER ALE 5.3% ABV
Biscuity, malty nose, with toasted caramel
in the middle and a balanced finish on the
sweet side of dry.

## Mothership Wit

WITBIER 4.8% ABV
The brewery's first organic beer. Fruity
and spicy; a creamy texture and wheat
tartness on the tongue. Refreshing acidity
at the finish.

# New Glarus

Highway 69, New Glarus,
Wisconsin 53574, **USA**
www.newglarusbrewing.com

In 2008, New Glarus Brewing
moved into a $21 million plant,
just outside a picturesque village
settled by Swiss pioneers in
1845. The attractive complex is
designed to look like a Wisconsin
dairy farm. In 2002 it was a
microbrewery that made 13,700
barrels; by 2007, it had increased
this fivefold. The expansion
allowed the brewery to double
production and keep pace with
the demand for brewmaster Dan
Carey's fruit beers and limited-
edition "Unplugged" brews.

### Spotted Cow
CREAM ALE 4.8% ABV
Faintly fruity, tasting of fresh peaches.
Pleasantly grainy, light on the tongue,
and refreshing.

### Fat Squirrel
BROWN ALE 5.5%
Hazelnuts on the nose, blending with
chocolate and caramel flavours; nicely
balanced by earthy hops.

# New Holland

690 Commerce Court, Holland,
Michigan 49423, **USA**
www.newhollandbrew.com

New Holland Brewing bottle
caps carry the slogan "Art in
Fermented Form", which
extends from beer to a line of
brandy-flavoured vodka, gin,
rum, and other spirits. To keep
up with demand for its assertive
beers, the brewery recently put
on line a used copper-domed
three-vessel brewhouse acquired
from Germany.

### The Poet

OATMEAL STOUT **6.5%** ABV
Abundant roast, chocolate, and dark,
rummy fruits. Full-bodied and creamy
enough to balance the coffee start.

### Black Tulip

TRIPLE **9%** ABV
Floral, with candy and honey sweetness,
and fruity notes. Sweet but tart in the
mouth, accented by spicy, bitter hops.

# Nils Oscar

Fruängsgatan 2, SE-611 31 Nyköping,
**SWEDEN**
www.nilsoscar.se

This microbrewery and distillery
was established in 1996 and
makes well-balanced beers that
go well with food. It has won
many awards, including four
medals in the World Beer Cup.

**BREWING SECRET** Nils Oscar has its
own maltings, and a farm where barley
and other cereals for malting are grown.

## Imperial Stout
IMPERIAL STOUT **7**% ABV
Well balanced and rich from ageing.
Chocolate aromas with caramel giving
way to a bittersweet finish.

## India Ale
INDIA PALE ALE **5.3**% ABV
Heavily hopped with Amarillo, giving an
aroma of tropical fruits; the fruitiness is
balanced by the crystal malt sweetness.

# Nøgne Ø

Gamle Rykene Kraftstasjon,
Lunde N-4885 Grimstad, **NORWAY**
www.nogne-o.com

Kjetil Jikiun launched Nøgne Ø
("naked island") in 2003 after
learning home-brewing in the
USA. Now his brewery is
Norway's largest supplier of
bottle-conditioned ale.

**BREWING SECRET** Nøgne mixes British
Marris Otter malt with American
C-hops, including Cascade, Centenneal,
Chinook, and Columbus.

### Saison
SAISON **6.5%** ABV
East Kent Goldings and Crystal hops
and Belgian ale yeast produce a light
and refreshing brew, available all year but
ideal in summer.

### Imperial Stout
IMPERIAL STOUT **9%** ABV
A dark, rich ale with a generous
sweetness and bitterness coming from
the roasted malts.

# North Coast

455 North Main Street, Fort Bragg,
California 95437, **USA**
www.northcoastbrewing.com

Since opening in 1988, North
Coast Brewing has cast a larger
shadow than its production levels
would suggest. Though small, it
sells beer in 36 states and exports
to Europe and the Pacific Rim
too. Brewmaster Mark Ruedrich
has further extended North
Coast's reputation by exploring
beer styles before many others.
Part of the profits from one,
Brother Thelonious, go to
the Thelonious Monk Institute
of Jazz.

### Old Rasputin
IMPERIAL STOUT **11.6%** ABV
Powerful, but flavourful – bitter and sweet
chocolate, burnt barley, rum, toffee, dried
dark fruits, espresso.

### Brother Thelonious
BELGIAN STRONG DARK ALE **9.3%** ABV
Spicy and candy-sweet aromas, with dark
fruits, notes of banana and caramelized
sugar, almost rummy.

# Oakham

Peterborough, Cambridgeshire,
PE2 7JB **ENGLAND**
www.oakhamales.com

Impressive growth from modest homebrew origins has led to the brewery now occupying its third site since 1993. The original owner sold the business on in 1995 but the early vision and ambitions prevail.

**BREWING SECRET** American hop varieties, with powerful floral characteristics, are a feature of the range.

### Jeffrey Hudson Bitter / JHB
BITTER **3.8**% ABV
Dominant citrus fruit hop aroma, which continues on the palate, blending into luscious malt flavours.

### White Dwarf
WHEAT BEER **4.3**% ABV
An English-style wheat beer, with flinty bitterness that mellows and reveals fruit nuances.

# Ochakovo

44, Riabinivaya, Moscow, **RUSSIA**
www.ochakovo.ru

Ochakovo is the last independent Russian brewery, and is trying to remain so. Its original brewhouse has been transformed into a museum, which takes visitors, step-by-step, through the brewing process and features many exhibits from the 19th century.

**BREWING SECRET** In 2005, Ochakovo launched an unpasteurized, unfiltered "live" beer, aimed at the health market.

## Ochakovo Classic
LAGER 5% ABV
Corn-yellow in colour, with intense malt overtones and a hoppy finish.

## Ochakovo Ruby
VIENNA LAGER 3.9% ABV
Pale ruby in colour, with aromas of winter fruits and floral notes, it has strong hints of caramel on the palate.

# Okell's

Douglas, Isle of Man,
IM2 1QG **ENGLAND**
www.okells.co.uk

Dr William Okell's steam-powered brewery – which he designed himself in 1874 – was regarded as one of the most sophisticated in the world at the time. Okell's new plant, which it moved to in 1994, is the modern equivalent. It is controlled by computers rather than steam, but the passion and commitment to quality beer production remains unaltered.

### Dr Okell's IPA

INDIA PALE ALE **4.4**% ABV
Potential sweetness, offset by a high hopping regime for overall roundness, spiced by lemon notes.

### Okell's Bitter

BITTER **3.7**% ABV
Light coloured and complexly flavoured, with hints of honey and a long-lingering dry finish.

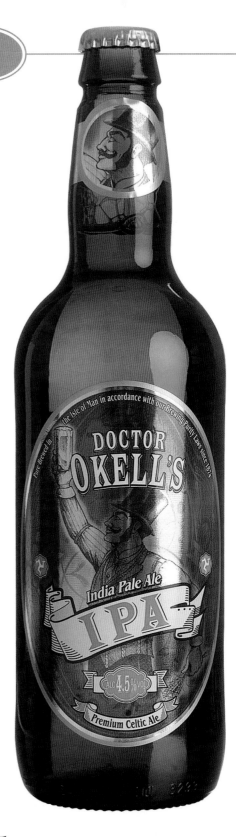

# Ommegang

656 County Highway 33,
Cooperstown, New York 13326, **USA**
www.ommegang.com

Owned by Belgium's Duvel
Moortgat, Brewery Ommegang
has brewed ales in the Belgian
tradition since 1997, selling
limited quantities across much
of the US. It hosts one of the
nation's most outstanding beer
festivals, Belgium Comes to
Coopers-town, each summer
in the picturesque brewery
grounds outside of town.

### Hennepin

SAISON 7.7% ABV
Spicy and peppery throughout. Yeasty
notes, citrus more apparent on the palate.
Tart and dry.

### Ommegang Abbey Ale

BELGIAN STRONG DARK ALE 8.5% ABV
The flagship ale, produced in the
spirit of a Christmas beer. Rich and
chocolatey, with underlying liquorice
and festive spices.

# Orkney

Stromness, Orkney,
KW16 3LT **SCOTLAND**
www.orkneybrewery.co.uk

Commendable ecological
awareness allows the brewery's
waste water to be filtered
through two neighbouring lochs
that support fish and waterfowl.
It was first set up in 1988, and
then thoroughly modernized
in 1994. Expansions in 2008
saw an increase in output and
the addition of a visitor centre
and shop.

### Dark Island
STRONG BITTER **4.6**% ABV
Ruby-red and mysterious, with
blackcurrant fruit on the nose
and a full-roasted malt palate.

### Skullsplitter
BARLEY WINE **8.5**% ABV
Forcefully malty nose; hints of
apple, spicy hop, and some nut
in the complex flavourings.

# Orval

2, Abbaye de Notre-Dame d'Orval,
B6823 Villers devant Orval,
**BELGIUM**
www.orval.be

The single Orval Trappist ale is a
symbol of the whole abbey: the
best in early 20th-century Art
Nouveau styling, blending with
the medieval ruins that surround
it. The bottle, glassware, and
everything else is designed with
an eye for beauty and peace. The
ruins can be visited, but alas, not
the newly revamped brewery.

## Orval

AMBER ALE **6.2%** ABV
An ultra dry ale that owes a large part of
its character to *Brettanomyces* yeasts,
(not unlike those that define lambic) and
to a high proportion of dry hops.

# Ostravar

Hornopolní 57, 728 25 Ostrava 1,
**CZECH REPUBLIC**
www.ostravar.cz

The Czech Republic's third-largest city lies closer to Katowice in Poland and Vienna in Austria than to Prague, and so prides itself on being "different" to other Czech breweries. Ostravar beers reflect this strategic position, and are carefully considered with local tradition in mind. It has, however, been internationally owned (now by InBev) since 2000.

### Ostravar Premium
PREMIUM LAGER **5.1**% ABV
A rich head promoting malt and hop aromas straddle a full-bodied strong bitter bite.

### Ostravar Kelt
STOUT **4.8**% ABV
Irish-style stout; pronounced hop and roasted barley aromas which continue throughout the palate.

# Otter Creek

793 Exchange Street, Middlebury, Vermont 05753, **USA**
www.ottercreekbrewing.com

The Wolaver family bought the well-established Otter Creek Brewery in 2002 in order to make its own organic ales, which had previously been made under contract at other breweries. Otter Creek beers are still produced as well, and the "World Tour" series includes Otter Mon (a Jamaican-style stout) and Otteroo (an Australian-style lager).

### Otter Creek Copper Ale
ALTBIER 5.4% ABV
Rich, complex, malty aromas and flavours, with a sneaky bitterness that extends the finish.

### Wolaver's Oatmeal Stout
OATMEAL STOUT 5.9% ABV
Chocolate and roasted coffee at the outset, blending with creamy notes in the mouth. Full-bodied, but finishing rather dry.

# Palmer's

Bridport, Dorset,
DT6 4JA **ENGLAND**
www.palmersbrewery.com

Palmer's is able to claim
continuous production on its
original site over a period of
more than 200 years. From the
outside it has altered little, but
this is a contemporary brewing
operation, offering a diverse
range of ales.

**BREWING SECRET** Maris Otter malted
barley and Golding hops combine to give
these beers their fruitiness.

### Traditional Best Bitter
BEST BITTER 4.2% ABV
Styled on an India Pale Ale; deliciously
hoppy, with fruit and malt undercurrents.

### Tally Ho!
STRONG BITTER 5.5% ABV
Distinctly nutty and dark, with full-bodied
complexity emerging slowly,
then on to a lingering afterglow.

# Panil (Torrechiara)

Strada Pilastro 35/a,
43010 Torrechiara (PR), **ITALY**
www.panilbeer.com

Renzo Losi, a biology graduate, got his brewing break in 2000, when his winemaker father gave him permission to make beer at the family's vineyard estate, south of Parma.

**BREWING SECRET** The links with the family winemaking tradition are retained in the use of oak barrels and *spumante* yeasts.

## Panil Barriquée Sour
FLEMISH SOUR RED 8% ABV
The flagship ale, barrel-aged for three months. Sour, vinous, and uncompromising.

## Divina
WILD BEER 5.5% ABV
Spontaneously fermented by being left, uncovered, on the back of a truck in a field overnight. Sweet-sour, yeasty, and citrusy.

# Pelican

33180 Cape Kiwanda Drive,
Pacific City, Oregon 97135, **USA**
www.pelicanbrewery.com

Set on the ocean shore,
Pelican lies just south of Cape
Kiwanda, one of Oregon's most
photographed landmarks.
Only small quantities are sold
outside the pub.

**BREWING SECRET** Its India Pelican
Ale and Doryman's Dark have both been
named Grand Champion Beer at the
Australian International Beer Awards.

### Doryman's Dark Ale
BROWN ALE 5.8% ABV
Complex malt qualities – roasted nuts,
cocoa, coffee beans, caramel – balanced
by Northwest hops.

### Tsunami Stout
STOUT 7% ABV
Deep black, with a creamy head. Coffee
and chocolate on the nose and palate,
rich and almost creamy. Pleasant acidic
bite at the end.

# Pete's

14800 San Pedro Avenue, San
Antonio, Texas 78232, **USA**
www.petes.com

Pete's Brewing was once
among the leading new wave
of American beer companies.
Founder Pete Slosburg sold the
business to San Antonio-based
Gambrinus in 1988, and the
brand has not matched the
success of other Gambrinus
companies. Brewed under
contract in New York, Pete's
is less widely available today.

### Pete's Wicked Ale
BROWN ALE 5.3% ABV

The defining American Brown Ale when
brewed to Slosberg's original homebrew
recipe lost its bite when the hopping rate
was halved.

### Wicked Strawberry Blond
FRUIT ALE 5% ABV

Looks more blond than strawberry, but
berry sweetness begins on the nose and
continues through the finish.

# Piccolo Birrificio

Via iv Novembre 20,
18035 Apricale (IM), **ITALY**
www.piccolobirrificio.com

This microbrewery, founded
in 2005, is housed in a former
olive-oil mill in the lovely
medieval village of Apricale,
near the French border. Brewer
Lorenzo Bottoni produces a
range of fine ales under the
brand name of Nüa ("naked"),
including some amazing
brews using unusual local
fruits and plants.

### Sesonette

BELGIAN SAISON **6.5**% ABV
Matured in Chardonnay barrels with
spices and local chinotto peel (from
a small, bitter citrus fruit).

### Chiostro

SPICED ALE **5**% ABV
Spiced with *Artemisia absinthium*
(wormwood), then fermented with
Trappist yeasts, giving complex and
unique aromas and flavours.

# Pietra

Route de la Marana,
20600 Furiani, **FRANCE**
www.brasseriepietra.com

The first Corsican brewery in history opened in 1996. Brewers Armelle and Dominique Sialelli use raw materials native to the island, such as *maquis* herbs and chestnut flour, which forms an ingredient rather than just a flavouring in their Pietra beer. *Biera Corsa* has been a great success, both in Corsica and overseas.

### Colomba

**WHEAT BEER 5% ABV**
Very fresh and sharp, with unusual aromas of arbutus, myrtle, and juniper. A refreshing summer beer.

### Pietra

**AMBER LAGER 6% ABV**
Elegant flavours of toasted malts, nuttiness, and a slight bitterness.

# Pilsner Urquell

U Prazdroje 7, 304 97 Plzeň,
**CZECH REPUBLIC**
www.pilsner-urquell.cz

The Czechs have blessed us
with the microwave oven, soft
contact lenses, and beer that
changed the world. It was,
however, a Bavarian who was
the key player in the Pilsner
Urquell story. As a young brewer,
Josef Groll presented the nation
with its first pilsner on 4 October
1842. This sensational clear
golden beer spread across
Europe like wildfire from its
"original source".

### Pilsner Urquell

CLASSIC PILSNER **4.4%** ABV
The ideal 35mm (one-and-a-half inch)
tight head leaves a lacing down the
glass with every sip of spiced leaf
and preserved fruit flavours, developing
a sweet malt piquancy and long,
enveloping finish.

# PRAGUE, CZECH REPUBLIC

The city of Prague is one of the world's greatest beer destinations. And where better to start a beer trail than in the Old Town Square (Staroměstské náměstí), location of the famous 15th-century Astronomical Clock – one of the world's oldest clocks still in working order. Many bars edge the square, each spilling out onto the pavements with seating and canopies.

### 2 U ZLATÉHO TYGRA

One of the Old Town's most atmospheric and oldest bars, U Zlatého Tygra is crowded with small tables, which always seem to be full with locals deep in energetic conversations – so be prepared to stand. It's a favourite of the writer and former Czech President Václav Havel, and President Clinton has also drunk here. The unfiltered Pilsner Urquell is said to be the best in Prague. *Husova 17, Prague*

### 1 OLD TOWN SQUARE

Here it is possible to sit outside and savour a beer, while watching the thousands of visitors who now flock to the Czech capital. Displays of folk dancing and music can often be enjoyed here too.

### 3 U PINKASŮ

In 1843 U Pinkasů was the first bar in Prague to serve Pilsner Urquell, and it is still available today. The bar was saved from extinction in 2000, when it was extensively refurbished. A more recent refurbishment has opened up more of the building. *Jungmannovo nám, 16/15, Prague*

## 5 PIVODUM

The Pivodum restaurant and bar is dominated by gleaming coppers. Traditional Czech beers are served, as well as other interesting brews, including a sour cherry beer, a coffee beer, and Samp – a beer champagne. Groups can order eight beers for the price of seven, and they are served in a large Giraffe-like container. A sample tray of eight beers is available too. *Ječná/Lípová 15, Prague*

## 4 NOVOMĚSTSKÝ PIVOVAR

An Art Deco-style entrance leads visitors down an alleyway of shops to this wood-panelled brewery, pub, and restaurant. Unfiltered light and dark beers are available. The food is unashamedly Czech, with specialities such as goulash, tripe soup, and roast knuckle of pork. *Vodickova 20, Prague*

## 6 U FLEKŮ

Crowded it may be, a haunt of many tourists it certainly is, but U Fleků should not be missed. Brewing began here in 1499, and it is said to be the world's oldest brewpub. It comprises many large rooms, including one for a booming oompah band. It has a small museum and daily brewery tours. The superb house beer is Flekovsky tmavy lezáck, which comes in dark and light versions. *Kremencova 11, Prague*

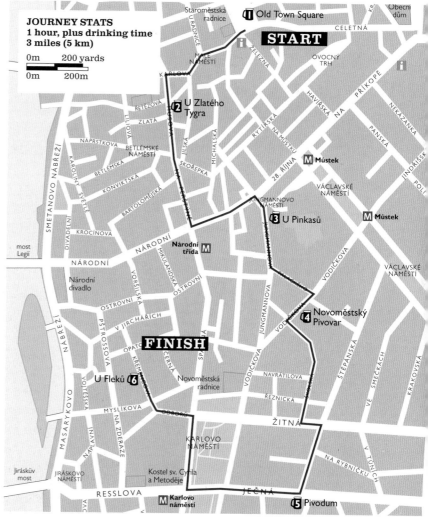

JOURNEY STATS
1 hour, plus drinking time
3 miles (5 km)

0m — 200 yards
0m — 200m

# De Prael

Helicopterstraat 13-15, 1059 CE
Amsterdam, **NETHERLANDS**
www.deprael.nl

Set up with the help of
government grants, Amsterdam's
smallest brewery has a workforce
made up of recovering
psychiatric patients. The first
choice of name – De Parel ("The
Pearl") – had to be changed
when Budels complained that
it infringed on the copyright
of their Parel beer. The solution
was simply to shuffle the letters
of the name around.

### Heintje
**WITBIER 5.4% ABV**
Unspiced, but with prominent citrus
aromas, a touch of fruit, and an
unexpectedly hoppy finish.

### Mary
**BARLEY WINE 9.6% ABV**
Neither malt nor hops dominate this
fruity strong ale, laced with pepper,
toffee, and caramel.

# Quilmes

Tte. Gral. Juan D. Peron 667 103,
Buenos Aires, **ARGENTINA**
www.quilmes.com.ar

The dominant beer in Argentina,
Quilmes is now part of the InBev
embrace. Like many breweries in
South America, it was begun by
a German, the brewery and malt
plant being founded in the 1880s
by Otto Bemberg. "Quilmes"
derives from an indigenous name
for the place where the brewery
is located.

### Quilmes Cristal
LAGER 4.9% ABV
Thin, pale and without any aromatic
distractions. Surprisingly drinkable,
though, with refreshing sweetness.

### Quilmes Stout
STOUT 4.8% ABV
Three malts clamour for attention –
but the expected coffee flavours are
overwhelmed by sweetness.

# Radegast

739 51 Nošovice, **CZECH REPUBLIC**
www.radegast.cz

Radegast, roughly meaning "dear guest", was the Slavic god of fertility and crops, and consequently became proclaimed god of hospitality too. Despite its nominal connections with the dawn of time, the brewery began operating only in 1970. It continues to be one of the country's most technologically advanced and best equipped beer producers.

### Radegast Original
PILSNER 4% ABV
A light malt and spiced hop nose, malt-sweet flavours and a crisp, grainy bitterness.

### Radegast Premium
PREMIUM LAGER 5% ABV
A characteristic herbal hoppy aroma and medium-sweet malt intensity dwell on cereal notes.

# Refsvindinge Brewery

Nyborgvej 80,
DK-5853 Ørbæk, **DENMARK**
www.bryggerietrefsvindinge.dk

Since 1885, four generations have run this farmhouse brewery. It was among the first to brew ales in Denmark and is credited with developing Danish white beer (*hvidtøl*) and the old-style smoked "ship's beer" (*skibsøl*), as well as two varieties of beer for children (not entirely alcohol free!).

### Ale No. 16
**BROWN ALE 5.7% ABV**
Well rounded, typical dark ale using original English yeast to produce a sweet, fresh taste.

### Mors Stout
**PORTER 5.7% ABV**
Dark, smooth porter brewed using malt that has been roasted with cocoa beans.

# Ridna Marka

71 Mikgorod str.Radomyshl,
**UKRAINE**
www.etalon-beer.com.ua/en

Beer making in Radomyshl dates from 1886, when this brewery was founded by the Czech Albrechtam brothers. They found that the soft water here was ideal for brewing. The modern brewery has adapted Bavarian technology to Ukrainian ingredients.

**BREWING SECRET** The brewhouse has been specifically designed to produce unfiltered, genuine wheat beers.

### Etalon Weissbier
**WHEAT BEER 5% ABV**
Spicy with a rich, creamy malt note and a long, quenching flavour and finish. Hints of bananas and vanilla.

# Robinson's

Stockport, Cheshire,
SK1 1JJ **ENGLAND**
www.frederic-robinson.co.uk

One of the British Isles' largest
regional breweries, Robinson's
began as the Union Inn in 1838.
Sixth-generation family members
are still in charge of its
development, overseeing huge
advances in brewing and
bottling techniques.

**BREWING SECRET** Tradition continues
here, and the brewery still uses its
surviving 1920s yeast strain.

### Old Tom Strong Ale
BARLEY WINE 8.5% ABV
Full-bodied with an aroma and flavour
alliance of malt, chocolate, fruit, and
port wine.

### Unicorn Best Bitter
BEST BITTER 4.2% ABV
Golden, with some spicy hop and
malt on the nose, countered by a
bittersweet release.

# Rochefort

8, Abbaye de Notre Dame de St-Remy,
B5580 Rochefort, **BELGIUM**
www.trappistes-rochefort.com

Though brewing has been
carried out here since 1900, it
is only since 1998 that Rochefort
has used labels on their bottled
beer. Recently, this smallest
of the Walloon Trappist
breweries decided to employ
a lay brewmaster, Gumer Santos,
to work on their beer production.
Since then, an amazing new
lagering room has begun taking
shape next to the abbey church,
and the few visitors allowed into
the abbey are now proudly shown
the new tasting room.

### Rochefort 6 (red)
ABBEY ALE **7.5%** ABV
Six is a veiled reference to the beer's
density (1060 OG) – and this lightest and
rarest Rochefort enjoys a very fruity taste.

### Rochefort 10 (blue)
ABBEY ALE **11.3%** ABV
A superior Trappist ale, with toffee,
chocolate, raisins, and port flavours,
and incomparable complexity.

# Rodenbach

Spanjestraat 133-141,
B8800 Roeselare, **BELGIUM**
www.rodenbach.be

The Rodenbach family started making beer in Roeselare in 1821. Now under the wing of Palm breweries, Rodenbach has turned resolutely modern, yet without doing away with its age-old traditions.

**BREWING SECRET** The "cathedral" of wooden fermenters is one of the most impressive sights in Belgian brewing.

## Rodenbach Classic

OUD BRUIN 5% ABV

Bearing the signs of its mixed fermentation and wood ageing, it is vinous in character and refreshing.

## Rodenbach Grand Cru

OUD BRUIN 6.5% ABV

A sour beer that has been aged in barrels: very severe and dry; one for the connoisseur.

# Rogue

2320 OSU Drive, Newport,
Oregon 97365, **USA**
www.rogueales.com

Rogue Ales has earned an international reputation for brewing envelope-pushing beers by creating a well-structured malt foundation on which to layer massive hop additions. This approach fostered the growth of the "Rogue Nation" – loyal fans who eagerly await the release of limited-edition beers.

**BREWING SECRET** Rogue beers are top-fermented using their own PacMan yeast which is well suited for bottle-conditioning.

## Shakespeare Stout

STOUT **6%** ABV

Dark, roasted chocolate and coffee mingle with dark fruits and husky malt. Substantial, balanced hops and an oily/creamy smooth finish.

## Dead Guy Ale

HELLER BOCK **6.6%** ABV

Complex, clean malt aromas, rich and fruity, becoming toastier on the palate. Bright bitter hops. Dry and spicy.

# Rooster's

Knaresborough, North Yorkshire,
HG5 8LJ **ENGLAND**
www.roosters.co.uk

The rules are simple:
unconditional care taken in the
selection and preparation of raw
materials is repaid in flavour.
Beer is not an alcoholic
commodity to master brewer
Sean Franklin, but a serious
sensory product, and inventive
infusions of lychees, roses,
coffee, grapefruit, and chocolate
are teased from hop varieties.

### Rooster's Yankee

BITTER **4.3**% ABV
Aromatic, softly bitter, with aromas
of tropical fruit and Muscat grapes
lingering alongside tangy malt.

### Outlaw Wild Mule

BITTER **3.7**% ABV
New Zealand hops create a Sauvignon
Blanc wine character in a remarkable
and imposing beer.

# Rothaus

Badische Staatsbrauerei Rothaus AG, Rothaus 1, 79865 Grafenhausen-Rothaus, **GERMANY**
www.rothaus.de

The Rothaus brewery was founded in 1791 by the Benedictine monastery St. Blasien. Today it is owned by the State of Baden-Württemberg and is one of the most profitable regional breweries in Germany. Although the brewery does not advertise, the Tannenzäpfle has become a cult brand in bars throughout Germany.

### Rothaus Tannenzäpfle

PILSNER 5.1% ABV
Tannenzäpfle ("little fir cones") is a crisp, elegant, well-rounded pilsner with a slight final bitterness.

### Rothaus Hefeweizen

WHEAT BEER 5.4% ABV
Refreshing top-fermented beer, with a mild fruity finish.

# Rouget de Lisle

Rue des Vernes,
39140 Bletterans, **FRANCE**
www.larougetdelisle.com

Opened in 2002, and named
after the locally born composer
of *The Marseillaise*, this brewery
develops up to 15 new beers each
year, some of them using local
ingredients instead of hops for
their bitter notes.

**BREWING SECRET** Among the
ingredients used to replace hops are
wormwood, dandelion, blackcurrant,
and gentian.

### Fourche Du Diable
LAGER 5.4% ABV
Amber in colour; aromas of spring
flowers and an unusual bitter note
contributed by gentian roots.

### Abisinthe
LAGER 6% ABV
Golden and very refreshing, with
aromas of mint, balm, and the special
bitterness of wormwood.

# Rulles

Artisanale de Rulles, 36, Rue Maurice Grevisse, B6724 Rulles, **BELGIUM**
www.larulles.be

Seldom does a brand new brewery (established only in 2000) meet with such immediate success. Grégory Verhelst's brews are mesmerizingly characterful, and the quality of the labels is equally amazing.

**BREWING SECRET** Grégory Verhelst enlisted the help of the Orval brewmaster to develop his beers.

## La Rulles Triple
BELGIAN PALE STRONG ALE 8.4% ABV
No lack of body here; herbal and dry-bitterness on the palate, yet well fermented and strong.

## La Rulles Estivale
SEASONAL ALE 5.2% ABV
A refreshing, citrusy, blossom-laden summer ale – one of the best of its kind.

# Russian River

1812 Ferdinand Court, Santa Rosa,
California 95404, **USA**
www.russianriverbrewing.com

Owner-brewmaster Vinnie
Cilurzo was the first to brew an
Imperial India Pale Ale
commercially, when he was at
Blind Pig Brewing. That beer is
now called Pliny the Elder and
has become the benchmark for
the style. Cilurzo and his wife,
Natalie, have built a production
brewery separate from their
popular downtown brewpub,
giving more space for a wider
range of barrels and ageing.

### Beatification

SOUR ALE **6**% ABV

A spontaneously fermented blended beer.
Complex, tart mix of fruit and wood. Just
right acidity at the finish.

### Pliny The Elder

IMPERIAL INDIA PALE ALE **8**% ABV

Hoppy aroma, hoppy flavour, and a
hoppy bitterness – all supported by
a firm malt base.

# Saint Arnold

2522 Fairway Park Drive, Houston,
Texas 77092, **USA**
www.saintarnold.com

The oldest surviving and largest
craft brewery in Texas was
founded in 1994. Saint Arnold
grew out of its "micro" status in
2007, although it continues to
sell its beer only within the state
borders. Austrian-born St Arnold
is one of the patron saints of
beer; the brewery's fermenters
are named after other saints.

## Amber

AMBER ALE **5.5%** ABV
Caramel and fermentation fruit, with
bright, spicy hops providing balance.
Excellent on cask.

## Elissa IPA

INDIA PALE ALE **6.6%** ABV
Delightfully hoppy throughout,
brimming with grapefruit character.
Big and juicy, with rich malt to match
the decided bitterness.

# Saint Germain

26 route d'Arras,
62160 Aix-Noulette, **FRANCE**
www.page24.fr

Two young but experienced
brewers opened this brewery in
2003, with top-fermentation
beers in the *bière de garde* style.
One takes its name from Saint
Hildegard, a German abbess of
the 11th century, who is often
(though incorrectly) credited
with the introduction of hops
into the beermaking process.

### Reserve Hildegarde Ambrée
ALE **6.9**% ABV
Golden, with a rich nose of cereals,
spices, and honey. Very smooth with
a good bitterness and a long finish.

### Page 24 Rhubarbe
ALE **5.9**% ABV
Gold in colour, with floral aromas.
Very refreshing, with a special acidity
contributed by rhubarb.

# Sainte-Hélène

21, Rue de la Colinne,
B6760 Ethe-Belmont, **BELGIUM**
www.sainte-helene.be

After a hectic start, this brewery really got going in 2005, when new brewing equipment was installed. The very southwest corner of Belgium seems to be particularly suited to brewing, as new breweries keep popping up there. Ste-Hélène is enthusiastic about promoting its beers, and is a regular at Belgium's many beer festivals.

### La Sainte Hélène Ambrée
BELGIAN AMBER STRONG ALE 8.5% ABV
Close in character to the triple, but with more caramel and tobacco notes; well-balanced.

### La Djean Triple
BELGIAN AMBER STRONG ALE 9% ABV
A beer with many flavours and impressions, from phenolic to fruity and dry to creamy.

# Samuel Adams

30 Germania Street, Boston,
Massachusetts 02130, **USA**
www.samueladams.com

The name Samuel Adams has been
synonymous with craft beer since
Boston Beer Company was one
of just a few speciality beer sellers
in the country. The company
launched the brand in 1984, when
it contracted production to
mainstream producers with excess
capacity. Boston Beer has since
purchased some of those
breweries and produces much of
its own beer. The company holds
an employees' homebrew contest
each year, with the winner's
beer being sold commercially.

### Boston Lager
VIENNA LAGER **4.9**% ABV
Complex flowery/piney nose. Full-bodied,
with caramel in the middle, and a
satisfyingly dry finish.

### Utopias
STRONG ALE **27**% ABV
The strongest beer in the world, aged in
brandy and port barrels. Serve and sip
like a rare cognac.

# Samuel Smith

High Street, Tadcaster, North Yorkshire, LS24 9SB **ENGLAND**
www.tadcaster.uk.com

Tadcaster has three breweries, with "Sam's" by far the smallest – although it can claim to be Yorkshire's oldest. A plentiful supply of water is drawn through limestone from its own wells.

**BREWING SECRET** Fermentation takes place in traditional slate "Yorkshire squares", which lends distinctive characteristics to flavour and body.

## Nut Brown Ale
BROWN ALE 5% ABV
A hazel-coloured speciality, with a flavour profile of beech nuts, almonds, and walnuts.

## Old Brewery Bitter
BEST BITTER 4% ABV
A typical Northern malty bitter, with a dash of hop and some fruit on the palate.

# Schlenkerla

Dominikaner Str. 6,
96049 Bamberg, **GERMANY**
www.schlenkerla.de

This legendary brewery was
known by 1405. Today it is still
a relatively small company, run
by a family in its sixth generation.
The so-called "smoked beer" is
a speciality of Bamberg.

**BREWING SECRET** The distinctive
smoky aroma of Schlenkerla's beers
comes from beechwood smoke that
pervades the malt as it dries above
the oven.

### Aecht Schlenkerla Rauchbier
MÄRZEN **5.1**% ABV
A very dark, dry beer. It has smoky and
roasted malt aromas and a finish of light
hops. A pure pleasure.

### Rauchbier Urbock
BOCK **6.5**% ABV
A traditional dark bock with
Schlenkerla's trademark smoky and
roasty aromas; dry, malty taste and
a good sweetness in the finish.

# BAMBERG, GERMANY

Can there be a better place in the world to drink beer? This beautiful, baroque island city, on the banks of the River Regnitz and the Main-Donau Canal, is in the Upper Franconia region of Bavaria. It is built on medieval foundations and is home to 70,000 people and 11 breweries. The city is a base for many US army personnel and their families – and they have helped, no doubt, to take the fame of this beer paradise around the world.

### 1 KLOSTERBRAU

Beer has been brewed at Klosterbrau since 1533. Down a cobbled street, time seems to slip away in this fairytale of a brewery tap. The range includes a schwarzbier, braunbier, weizen, pils, and a bock. *Oberre Muhlbruck 3, Bamberg (www.klosterbraueu.de)*

### 2 OLD TOWN HALL

The river is never far away in Bamberg. The stroll to Brauerei Spezial's passes the spectacular medieval stone-and-timbered Old Town Hall, which seems precariously balanced on the footings of an ancient bridge. Take a moment to admire it before heading on to the Brauerei Spezial's.

### 3 THE BRAUEREI SPEZIAL'S

The Brauerei Spezial's is very much a locals' bar, decorated with laughter and conversations. Its Specizil Rauchbier has subtle, soft toffee flavours and even a hint of burnt straw. Spezial uses smoked malt in at least four of its other beers. By the bar is a serving hatch, where locals come to fill containers with beer for drinking at home. *Obere Königstrasse 10, Bamberg (www.brauerei-spezial.de)*

### 4 BRAUEREI FÄSSLA

Directly opposite Brauerei Spezial's is Brauerei Fässla. Brewing started here in 1649. The brewery tap has a comfortable, wood-panelled, country-style room, and above it is a small hotel. The brewery's logo – a dwarf rolling a barrel of beer – decorates the glasses and dark furniture. Fässla's easy-drinking Lagerbier melds malty flavours with a fresh, soft bitterness. *Obere Königsstrasse 19–21, Bamberg (www.faessla.de)*

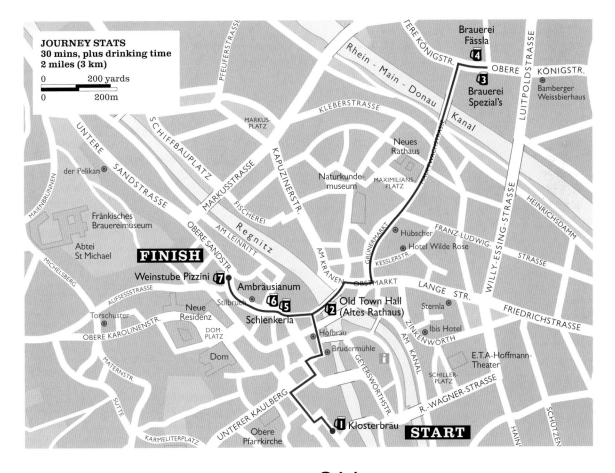

### 6 AMBRÄUSIANUM

Opposite Schlenkerla is the Ambräusianum. Here, the brewing vessels can been seen, which makes it seem more like a modern brewpub than one of Bamberg's traditional establishments, and it is a relative newcomer, being open only since 2004. Weekend breakfasts comprise a glass of wheat beer with three locally made Bavarian veal sausages and a pretzel. *Dominikanerstrasse 10, Bamberg (www.ambraeusianum.de)*

### 5 SCHLENKERLA

Vibrant and friendly, Schlenkerla is Bamberg's best-known bar and restaurant. The warmth of its world-famous rauchbier, with its smoked whisky and cheese overtones, is as warm as the welcome. Tables are often shared, and the atmosphere is highly convivial. Beer is the social lubricant and the perfect accompaniment to robust Bavarian dishes such as onions stuffed with beery meatballs. *Dominikanerstrasse 6, Bamberg (www.smokebeer.com)*

### 7 WEINSTUBE PIZZINI

The exterior of the Weinstube Pizzini is somewhat unprepossessing, and do not be deterred by its name – it is neither a wine bar nor a pizza restaurant. Inside this small, brown decorated and time-worn bar, there is warm-hearted welcome and the opportunity to try Fässla and Spezial beers, as well as a dunkel from Andechser. *Ober Sandstrasse 17, Bamberg*

**JOURNEY STATS**
30 mins, plus drinking time
2 miles (3 km)

0 — 200 yards
0 — 200m

# Schneider

Private Weissbierbrauerei Schneider,
Emil-Ott-Str. 1-5, 93309 Kelheim,
**GERMANY**
www.schneider-weisse.de

The Schneider brewery has been
a family-owned company since it
was founded. From its original
location in Munich, Schneider
moved to Kelheim after World
War II. The former brewery in
central Munich has since become
a world-famous restaurant.

## Schneider Weisse Original

WHEAT BEER 5.4% ABV

People call it "liquid amber", and they
are right: the amber-mahogany colour is
beautiful. Fresh, full-bodied, and with
a light bitter finish.

## Aventinus

STRONG WHEAT BEER 8.2% ABV

Almost black, legendary beer, with
chocolate and dried-fruit aromas;
full-bodied, very thick, and fresh.

# Schwechater

Mautner Markhof-Strasse 11, A-2320
Schwechat, **AUSTRIA**
www.schwechater.at

A large brewery that claims to
have brewed the first lager beer
in 1840, though, to be precise, it
was the Vienna lager that was
invented here by Anton Dreher.
Production of that beer was
discontinued in the early 20th
century. Nowadays the brewery
is part of Heineken and produces
golden lagers.

### Schwechater Zwickl

**UNFILTERED PILSNER 5.5% ABV**
Herbal hop aromas and a hint of lemon
zest. A lot of wheat in the mash bill. Dry
and hoppy finish.

### Schwechater Bier

**PALE LAGER 5% ABV**
Golden colour, malty aromas. Full-bodied
with hops being noticeable from the start
to the finish.

# Sharp's

Wadebridge, Cornwall,
PL27 6NU **ENGLAND**
www.sharpsbrewery.co.uk

Facing the Atlantic from the
Cornish coast undoubtedly has
an influence, not only on how
the beer is made, but also on
people's objectives and horizons.
Sharp's commendable approach
to sustainable energy and water
recycling is echoed by an
energetic attitude, which is
inspiring for the future of
cask ale production.

## Doom Bar

BITTER 4% ABV
Spicy resinous hop aromas and sweet,
delicate malts blend with dried fruit
and assertive bitterness.

## Atlantic IPA

INDIA PALE ALE 4.8% ABV
Four hop varieties are added at different
stages to create candyfloss aromas and
crisp, delicate flavours.

# Shepherd Neame

Faversham, Kent,
ME13 7AX **ENGLAND**
www.shepherdneame.co.uk

It didn't take 12th-century monks long to discover that Faversham's pure spring water could be combined with locally grown malting barley to produce particularly fine ale. When the town's mayor founded a brewery in 1698, he launched the country's longest-surviving brewery, which was by 1864 called Shepherd Neame. Still run by the Neame family.

**BREWING SECRET** The brewery still makes use of mash tuns made from Russian teak, installed in 1914.

### Bishop's Finger
STRONG BITTER 5% ABV
Generously fruity, with banana and pear prominent, a biscuit-rich maltiness, and dried fruit flavours.

### Spitfire
PREMIUM BITTER 4.5% ABV
A underlying deep maltiness is combined with a subtle hint of toffee and boldly fruity citrus hops.

# Shiga Kogen

1163 Hirao, Yamanouchi-machi,
Shimo Takai-gun Nagano 381-0401,
**JAPAN**
www.tamamura-honten.co.jp

In September 2004, saké brewer
Tamamura Honten broke a little
of their 200-year tradition and
began brewing beer. Within three
years Shiga Kogen had become
one of the most respected
Japanese craft beer brands. Clear
product identity and superior
label designs have contributed
to the beer's popularity.

### House DPA / Draft Pale Ale
PALE ALE 8% ABV
American in style, with a brilliant
orange-gold hue, complex floral hop
aroma, and lingering sweetness.

### Miyama Blonde
SAISON-LIKE BEER 7% ABV
Made using the Miyama Nishiki strain
of saké rice, along with European
hops and barley. Rich and interesting,
but with a brisk finish.

# Shiner

603 Brewery Street, Shiner,
Texas 77984, **USA**
www.shiner.com

Founded in 1909, the Spoetzl
Brewery has ridden the success
of Shiner Bock into national
prominence. In 2004 it began
counting down toward its 100th
birthday by releasing a special
new beer every year, each one
reflecting a German heritage that
dates back to the original Shiner
Brewing Association.

## Shiner Hefeweizen

HEFEWEIZEN **5.3**% ABV
Cloudy, brewed in Bavarian style with a
little honey. More wheat character than
yeast, with citrus hints.

## Shiner Bock

US DARK LAGER **4.4**% ABV
A dark lager, rather than a true German
bock. Hints of caramel sweetness.
Deliberately low on hops.

# Shongweni / Robson's

B1 Shongweni Valley, Shongweni, near Durban, KwaZulu-Natal, **SOUTH AFRICA**
www.shongwenibrewery.com

Shongweni mainly produces bottle-conditioned beers, using the infusion mash technique and fermentation in open-top vessels. All its beers are unfiltered and unpasteurized. The family-owned brewery stands out in a local market dominated by mass-produced lagers. It exports to the UK and elsewhere.

### Robson's Durban Pale Ale
INDIA PALE ALE 5.7% ABV
Brewed with Pale malt, and Cascade and Challenger hops. Crisp, fruity, and well-balanced.

### Robson's East Coast Ale
GOLDEN ALE 4% ABV
A smooth and refreshing golden ale, made with a single malt variety along with Brewers Gold and Challenger hops.

# Siebensternbräu

Siebensterngasse 19,
A-1070 Vienna, **AUSTRIA**
www.7stern.at

Siebensternbräu was the first brewpub in Austria to brew speciality beers – IPA, chilli, and fruit flavoured. Owner Sigi Flitter also helped re-introduce many of Austria's indigenous but forgotten beer styles.

**BREWING SECRET** The range varies with each season, but expect a wheat beer in summer and a smoked in winter.

### Rauchbock
SMOKED BOCK **7.9%** ABV
Intense smoky nose; full, almost sweet, body, with hints of chocolate and liquorice, and a smoky finish.

### Prager Dunkles
DARK LAGER **4.5%** ABV
While most dark beers in Austria are terribly sweet, this one is dry. Intense toasty notes, very little hop aroma. Roasty finish.

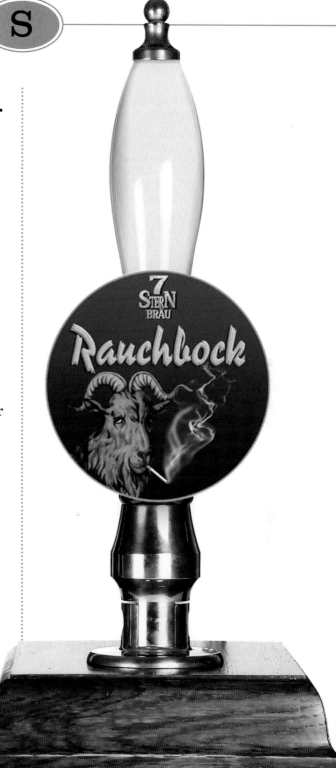

# Sierra Nevada

1075 East 20th Street, Chico,
California 95928, **USA**
www.sierranevada.com

Sierra Nevada Brewing has been
introducing beer drinkers to
citrusy, piney Northwest hops
since 1981, and the brewery
continues to act as a matchmaker
between beer drinkers and hops.
Sierra Nevada is also an industry
leader in good environmental
practice. It has commissioned the
first phase of one of the country's
largest private solar installations,
which will bring it close to its
goal of generating 100 per cent of
its energy needs.

### Pale Ale
PALE ALE 5.6% ABV
Piney, grapefruity Cascade hops play
against malt fruitiness on both the nose
and the palate.

### Bigfoot
BARLEY WINE 9.6% ABV
Earthy and chewy, with prominent citric
hops and whisky-like rich malts. Boldly
bitter when young.

# Silly / Mynsbrug Hen

2, Ville Basse, B7830 Silly, **BELGIUM**
www.silly-beer.com

Established in the 19th century, this family brewery walks a fine line between maintaining traditions and employing technical developments geared towards satisfying changing market niches. A *saison* is still produced – bottled and, better yet, on draught – and they have recently launched a beer flavoured with rum and named after a regional rock band.

### Silly Saison

SAISON 5.2% ABV

Fruity, madeira-like, thin-bodied. Even when young, this is more like an oud bruin than a real *saison*.

### Scotch Silly

SCOTCH ALE 8% ABV

Scotch ales are a Walloon tradition. This very malty dark beer is full-bodied and rich.

# Simonds Farsons Cisk

The Brewery, Notabile Road,
Mriehel, BKR 01, **MALTA**
www.farsons.com

Wherever the British army went, beer was soon to follow, and this brewery was built in lavish Art Deco style at the end of World War II in 1946. The site is being redeveloped, with the old brewing vessels at the heart of a visitor centre.

**BREWING SECRET** It brews the potent XS (9% ABV) for the export market.

### Farsons Lacto
MILK STOUT 3.8% ABV
Soft on the tongue, this black beer is a classic milk stout, with lactose added after fermentation.

### Hopleaf Extra
ALE 5% ABV
English malt, along with Challenger and Target hops, produce a complex beer with a refreshing bitter finish.

# Sinebrychoff

Oy Sinebrychoff Ab,
Sinebrychoffinaukio 1 PL 87,
FL-04201 Kerava, **FINLAND**
www.koff.fi

Sinebrychoff is part of the
Carlsberg Group, and its
abbreviated name and main
brand range, Koff, is one of the
most popular in Finland. It is the
oldest Nordic brewery, founded
by Russian Nikolai Sinebrychoff
in 1819.

**BREWING SECRET** Karhupanimo, their
new microbrewery, is producing a range
of hand-crafted lagers.

### Sinebrychoff Porter
IMPERIAL STOUT **7.2**% ABV
Robust and brimming with coffee
flavours, this beer has a long,
warming finish.

### Karhu III
LAGER **4.6**% ABV
Described by the brewer as "untamed".
Full-bodied, with stronger flavours of
hops and malt than are usual for a lager.

# Ska

545 Turner Drive, Durango,
Colorado 81301, **USA**
www.skabrewing.com

Bill Graham and Dave Thibodeau
named their brewery for the
Jamaican music they played
while homebrewing in college,
reflecting their motto "it takes
characters to brew beer with
character". When they founded
Ska in 1995, they had day jobs
and brewed at night. Now they
can't keep up with the demand
for their beers and are building
a new brewery.

## Ten Pin Porter

**PORTER 5.4% ABV**
Chocolate and caramel throughout, with
roasted coffee stronger in the flavour.
Eases into bitterness.

## True Blonde

**GOLDEN ALE 4.2% ABV**
Brewed with honey made just north of
town. Light biscuity malt, hints of honey
and a touch of citric hops.

# Sleeman

551 Clair Road West, Guelph,
Ontario, N1L 1E9, **CANADA**
www.sleeman.com

The Sleeman family started
brewing in Canada in 1834, the
year John Sleeman, an ambitious
young brewer from England,
arrived in Ontario. In 1851
he started the first Guelph-based
Sleeman Brewery, making small,
100-barrel batches with local well
water, prized for its purity and
hardness. The company is now
owned by Sapporo.

### Honey Brown Lager

LAGER 5% ABV

A refreshingly smooth, full-bodied lager,
with a subtle touch of honey which
creates a slightly sweet finish.

### Sleeman Cream Ale

ALE 5% ABV

Designed to combine the refreshing
quality of German lager with the
distinctive taste of English Ale.

# Smuttynose

225 Heritage Avenue, Portsmouth,
New Hampshire 03801, **USA**
www.smuttynose.com

Although Smuttynose Brewing
has earned a reputation for its
carefully balanced offerings, the
brewery was also one of the first
to embrace "extreme beers",
launching a Big Beer Series in
1998. Succeeding on all fronts, it
found itself out of room by 2007,
and plans to relocate its brewing,
still close to Portsmouth.

### Shoals Pale Ale

PALE ALE 5% ABV

First made at the Portsmouth pub.
Pleasant fruity/biscuit palate gives
way to a crisp American hop finish.

### Robust Porter

PORTER 5.7% ABV

Rich dark fruits and chocolate, well
blended throughout. Rich, roasty flavours
leave a strong impression for a medium-
strength beer.

# Snake River

265 S. Millward Street, Jackson,
Wyoming 83001, **USA**
www.snakeriverbrewing.com

Located in central Jackson, with
a view of Snow King Mountain
and standing but a few miles
from the Jackson Hole ski resort,
Snake River brewpub occupies
an old cinder-block warehouse.
It has twice won Small Brewery
of the Year at the Great American
Beer Festival.

### Zonker Stout
STOUT **5.8**% ABV
Roasted barley sets a bold tone, with
chocolate (almost sweet) underneath.
Pleasingly dry finish.

### Lager
VIENNA LAGER **6**% ABV
Golden, with a thick white head.
Malt-accented, clean toasted and
caramel flavours, drying hop finish.

# Southampton

40 Bowden Square, Southampton,
New York 11968, **USA**
www.publick.com

Southampton Publick House's
busy brewmaster, Phil
Markowski, routinely travels
to three breweries in New York
State and Pennsylvania to make
Southampton-branded beer.
As well as the eclectic range he's
created for the brewery-restaurant
on Long Island, he also brews
specials, packaged in 750ml
corked bottles, and oversees the
production of Double White and
Secret Ale. Since early 2008, the
Southampton range of beers has
been marketed by Pabst.

### Saison
SAISON 6.5% ABV
An endorsement for "Farmhouse Ales"
– fruity, peppery, slightly tart, earthy,
and refreshing.

### Secret Ale
ALTBIER 5.1% ABV
Slightly sweet caramel aromas, with firm
bitterness matching rich malt on the
palate, lasting beyond the finish.

# Starobrno

Hlinky 160/12, 661 47 Brno,
**CZECH REPUBLIC**
www.starobrno.cz

Brewing around Brno began in
monasteries and convents,
notably those of the Augustinian
Brothers and Cistercian Sisters.
The highest production and
technical standards – features
of its Mandell and Huzak family
ownership since 1872 – have
earned Starobrno a coveted
"Czech Made" quality
certificate. It is now owned
by Dutch firm Heineken.

### Starobrno Premium Lager

**PREMIUM LAGER 4% ABV**
A nose of hay, melon, and malt,
then heightening traces of caramel
on the palate.

### Starobrno Rezák

**DARK BEER 4% ABV**
A deep amber Vienna-style lager
unveiling slight bitter hop and joyous
caramel mouthfuls.

# Staropramen

Nádražni 84, 150 54 Prague 5,
**CZECH REPUBLIC**
www.staropramen.com

Far-sighted developers situated the Smíchov Brewery in Prague's future industrial area, where demand for beer was assured. From the start, Staropramen – Prague's biggest brewer – was perceived as a Czech beer for Czech people, which gave it an advantage amongst nationalist-leaning consumers. Today it is owned by global giant InBev.

### Staropramen Dark Beer
DARK BEER **4.5%** ABV
Its light body loops around malty caramel, liquorice, and aniseed notes to a floral finale.

### Staropramen Premium Lager
PREMIUM LAGER **5%** ABV
A rich floral bite unveils a full-bodied satisfier with a *riz* ("just right") finish.

# St Austell

St Austell, Cornwall,
PL25 4BY **ENGLAND**
www.staustellbrewery.co.uk

The enterprising spirit that drove Walter Hicks to mortgage his farm for £1,500 in 1851 and set up a brewery remains at the core of today's business. Many of his descendants are still involved in the company – in its estate of 168 pubs and in the brewery, which produces in excess of 40,000 barrels (6.5 million litres) annually.

## Tribute
BITTER 4.2% ABV
Specially grown Cornish Gold barley delivers a rich biscuit aroma, tempered by intense fruit flavours.

## St Austell IPA
INDIA PALE ALE 3.4% ABV
Full of flavour and packed with fresh hoppiness; the rounded palate arrives with veils of caramel.

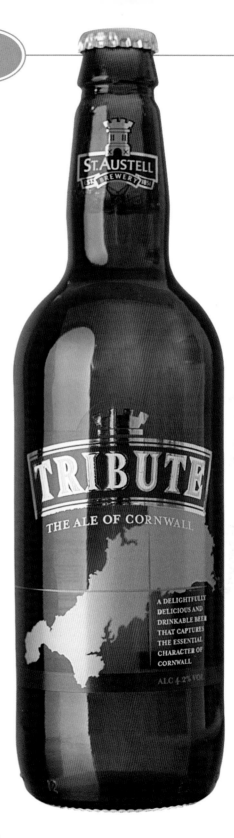

# St Christoffel

Metaalweg 10, 6045 JB Roermond, **NETHERLANDS**
www.christoffelbier.nl

Operating since 1986, St Christoffel is one of the oldest Dutch micros, founded (but no longer run) by Leo Brand, a member of the Brand brewing dynasty. It produces the very best lagers brewed in the Netherlands.

**BREWING SECRET** The Robertus beer is a rare example of a Münchner dark lager that's true to the Bavarian style.

## Christoffel Blond
### PILS 6% ABV
Spicy hop flavours burst from the glass – basil, mint, ginger, grapefruit, and cloves are all there.

## Christoffel Robertus
### MÜNCHNER 6% ABV
The nutty flavour of Munich malt runs right through this beer, flanked by biscuit, toast, and toffee.

# Stiegl

Kendlerstrasse 1,
A-5017 Salzburg, **AUSTRIA**
www.stiegl.at

Austria's largest independent brewery produces Austria's single most successful beer, Goldbräu. The brewery itself dates back to 1492 and, over time, has built up a splendid collection of beer-related exhibits for the "Brauwelt" – the largest museum on the continent entirely devoted to brewing.

### Goldbräu
AUSTRIAN MÄRZEN-TYPE
LAGER **4.9%** ABV
Relatively low bitterness and a hint of malty sweetness in the aroma and on the palate.

### Paracelsus Zwickl
ORGANIC LAGER **5%** ABV
Unfiltered, so hazy orange in hue; aromas of malt and yeast; medium body and very low bitterness.

# Brauhaus Sternen

Hohenzornstrasse 2, CH-8500
Frauenfeld, **SWITZERLAND**
www.brauhaussternen.ch

This is an intriguing brewpub,
set up on the site of the
Aktienbrauerei Frauenfeld,
where Martin Wartmann created
Ittinger (now brewed at Calanda).
The present brewery was built
in 2003 with financial help from
many prominent European
brewers eager to see Martin
brew interesting beers, some
in limited editions ("Nur für
Freunde" – "for friends only").

### Wartmann's Nur Für Freunde No1

BELGIAN DUBBEL 9.6% ABV

Chocolaty, slightly sweet aroma. Full-
bodied and fruity (ripe plums); very mild
bitterness in the finish.

### Honey Brown Ale

BROWN ALE 6% ABV

Sweet and fruity. Quite refreshing for its
strength. Very low bitterness and a hint
of honey in the finish.

# Stiftsbrauerei Schlägl

Schlägl 1, A-4160 Schlägl, **AUSTRIA**
www.stift-schlaegl.at

The small village of Schlägl, close to the Czech and Bavarian borders, is home to the only Austrian brewery wholly owned by a monastery – in this case the Premonstratensian order. In recent years the product range has grown considerably and now includes several ales.

### Stifter Bier
RED ALE **5.7%** ABV
Malty sweetness with a refreshing fruit (peach and melon) undertone. Just a faint hint of hops.

### Doppelbock
DOPPELBOCK **8.3%** ABV
A big, malty nose. Fruity (pears and apples) and sweet from the start, but very well-balanced finish.

# Švyturys-Utenos

Kuliu Vartu g. 7, Klaipeda,
**LITHUANIA**
www.svyturys.lt/en

Brewing began here in 1784, making this the oldest brewery in Lithuania. The company has a reputation for the quality of its beers and has won several international brewing awards. It is open to the public for tours twice a week for groups of five to 25 (via the tourist office at www. klaipedainfo.lt).

**BREWING SECRET** All the employees give their feedback on each new brew.

### Švyturys Ekstra
DORTMUND LAGER 5.2% ABV
Clear and golden, it has a firm white head, an intense aroma of hops and a slight bitterness.

### Švyturio
LAGER 5% ABV
Translucent gold in colour, it has a good balance of rich malt and bitter hops. In Lithuania it's known simply as "red", due to its label colour.

# Teerenpeli

Hämeenkatu 19, Lahti, **FINLAND**
www.teerenpeli.com

Teerenpeli operates breweries, bars, and restaurants in Helsinki, Lahti, and Tampere. Its first brewery was founded in 1995. A new brewery and whisky distillery opened in 2002, set within the Restaurant Taivaanranta in Lahti. Teerenpeli's beers have won medals at the Helsinki Beer Festival.

## Laiskajaakko

DARK LAGER **4.5%** ABV
Full-bodied, malty dark lager, brewed with Crystal 50 and Black malt, and Hallertau hops.

## Onnenpekka

PALE LAGER **4.7%** ABV
Golden and refreshing. Made with Pilsner barley malt from the Lahti region, and pure water from the Salpausselkä area.

# Terrapin

255 Newton Bridge Road, Athens, Georgia 30607, **USA**
www.terrapinbeer.com

Spike Buckowski and John Cochran began shipping beer from their own brewhouse early in 2008, almost six years after the Terrapin Beer Company started selling contract-brewed Rye Pale Ale. That beer was an immediate hit, as was the Monster Beer Tour, a series of strong beers released after Georgia raised its 6 per cent ABV cap on beer.

### Rye Pale Ale
PALE ALE 5.3% ABV
Rye blends with bright grapefruit, adds texture to fruit fermentation, and complements late bitterness.

### Wake-n-Bake Coffee Oatmeal Imperial Stout
IMPERIAL STOUT 8.1% ABV
It's all in the name, along with chocolate-covered dark fruits.

# Theakston

Masham, North Yorkshire,
HG4 4YD **ENGLAND**
www.theakstons.co.uk

Ownership battles may have
swept in numerous changes
during its 180-year history but,
fortunately today, tradition
survives and thrives. Now
returned to the Theakston
family following Scottish &
Newcastle's management, the
company lives up to the name
of its most famous beer –
Peculier, a 12th-century word
meaning "particular".

### Old Peculier
STRONG BITTER **5.6**% ABV
Rich and deep dark ruby in hue, with
a mellow fruit aroma and a malty,
full-bodied flavour.

### Black Bull Bitter
BITTER **3.9**% ABV
Bright amber coloured, with a crisp
dry palate weaving through citrus
fruit flavours.

# Thiriez

22 rue de Wormhout,
59470 Esquelbecq, **FRANCE**
http://brasseriethiriez.ifrance.com

From working as a manager in a food distribution company, Daniel Thiriez changed his life to become an artisan brewer. He established his brewery on an old farm in Flanders in 1996, and uses traditional brewing methods.

**BREWING SECRET** Thiriez's unfiltered beers have a second fermentation in the bottle, on their lees.

## Étoile Du Nord
**BLOND ALE 5.5% ABV**
The moment the bottle is opened, an extraordinary smell of fresh hops comes to the nose. The beer's refreshing bitterness is in perfect harmony with its fine malt aromas.

# Thornbridge

Bakewell, Derbyshire,
DE45 1NZ **ENGLAND**
www.thornbridgebrewery.co.uk

Resounding success has followed from the brewery's philosophy of being "never ordinary". While brewing heritage is of prime importance, innovation, enthusiasm, experience, and a commitment to creating new and exciting recipes have driven the business since it was established in 2005 in the grounds of Thornbridge Hall country manor house.

### Jaipur

INDIA PALE ALE 5.9% ABV
Tantalizingly complex; emphasis on citrus hoppiness; its powerful length develops a bitter finish.

### Lord Marples

BITTER 4% ABV
Easy-drinking bitter, with hints of honey and caramel, and a long, bitter afterglow.

Three Boys Wheat beer evokes ancie[...]
when yeasts were wild and spices in[...]
were added for bitterness. We use g[...]
yeast that with the wheat malt produc[...]
frothy head, cloudiness and huge flavo[...]
this wit bier (white beer) style. The add[...]
and citrus zest really make this beer sp[...]

500mL

three boys

Wheat

Batch No:
1072

# Three Boys Brewery

Unit 10, Garlands Rd, Woolston, Christchurch, **NEW ZEALAND**
www.threeboysbrewery.co.nz

Microbiologist Ralph Bungard employs a broad range of yeasts to produce tasty Kiwi interpretations of classic beer styles. The senior "Boy" – the others are his sons Marek and Quinn.

**BREWING SECRET** The brewery's limited release seasonal brews include an excellent Oyster Stout in winter and a fragrant Golden Ale in summer.

## Three Boys Wheat
WITBIER 5% ABV
Plenty of zesty lemon and coriander notes, with a hint of ginger. A spritzy and quenching brew.

## Three Boys Porter
ROBUST PORTER 5.2% ABV
Rich mocha notes dominate a silky palate, while heavily roasted grain and hops compete in the dry finish.

# Three Floyds

9750 Indiana Parkway, Munster,
Indiana 46321, **USA**
www.threefloyds.com

Beginning with its flagship
Alpha King in 1996, Three Floyds
Brewing had lived by
the philosophy of brewmaster
Nick Floyd: "I love the smell of
hops in the morning. It smells
like victory."

**BREWING SECRET** The annual release
of Dark Lord Russian Imperial Stout
sells out in one day, with customers
driving hundreds of miles to buy it.

## Alpha King
PALE ALE 6% ABV
Opens with a rush of citrus fruits. Firm
malt backbone, matched by hop oils.
Prolonged bitterness.

## Gumballhead
US WHEAT BEER 4.8% ABV
Citrus and orchard fruits on the
nose, followed by wheat tartness
and hops throughout.

# Timmermans

Kerkstraat 11, B1701 Itterbeek,
**BELGIUM**
www.anthonymartin.be/Public/

Once a traditional lambic
brewery, Timmermans was
among the first to habitually
mix top-fermented beer into its
blends. The brewery has also
been keen to produce all kinds
of syrup-lambic concoctions,
designed to appeal more to
the younger generation.
Timmermans products, including
Tradition, are easily found in
Belgian supermarkets.

### Tradition Gueuze
GUEUZE 5% ABV
Once known as "Caveau", this beer is a
mix of tradition and commercialism, and
so are its flavours: more pineapple than
citrus, and herbal rather than the typical
horse blanket notes.

# Timothy Taylor

Keighley, West Yorkshire,
BD21 1AW **ENGLAND**
www.timothy-taylor.co.uk

The Taylor family guides the
enterprise, as it has done since
the brewery's inception in 1858.

**BREWING SECRET** Pure Pennine water
from the brewery's own spring is a
natural companion to the Golden Promise
barley (also used extensively for malt
whisky); together, they form the
legendary "Taylor's taste".

## Landlord

PREMIUM BITTER **4.3%** ABV
Complex hoppy aroma, well-balanced
spice and citrus fruit flavours, tinged
with biscuit malt.

## Best Bitter

BEST BITTER **4%** ABV
A full measure of maltiness following
citrus fruit, hoppy aromas define an
honest Yorkshire bitter.

# Titanic

Burslem, Staffordshire,
ST6 1JL **ENGLAND**
www.titanicbrewery.co.uk

What began with brewing for demonstration purposes on log-fired Victorian equipment developed into the production of in excess of 17 million pints a year. Ecologically friendly business practices – recycling and conservation – are a priority. The name is taken from the world's most famous passenger ship, whose captain, John Edward Smith, was born nearby.

### Titanic Stout

STOUT **4.5% ABV**

Full roast, preserved fruit aromas; the malt-influenced palate accentuates more fruit and liquorice tiers.

### Best Bitter

BEST BITTER **3.5% ABV**

Straw coloured, with a waft of sulphur in the aroma and persistent hop flavourings.

# Topvar

Krusovska cesta 2092,
Topolcany, **SLOVAKIA**
www.topvar.sk

The brewery operates at two
sites in Slovakia: Topolcany
and Velký Šariš. In 2000, the
brewery launched a beer called
Brigita, named after the Slovak
finance minister Brigita
Schmögnerovà. A popular beer,
it remained on sale for some
time after her resignation
in 2002. The company is now
owned by SABMiller.

### Topvar Svetlé

LAGER 5.2% ABV

A sunburst of yellow tones, with a thin
white head. This beer has an attractive
nose, with plenty of citrus fruit flavours.

# Traquair

Innerleithen, Peeblesshire,
EH44 6PW **SCOTLAND**
www.traquair.co.uk

The 18th-century brewing
equipment in a house where
Bonnie Prince Charlie once
sought refuge remained
untouched until their rediscovery
in 1965. Since then, they have
been put to use for brewing in
authentic style.

**BREWING SECRET** Unusually in this
day and age, Traquair's beers are
fermented in oak over a seven-day period.

### Traquair House Ale
BARLEY WINE **7.2%** ABV
A dark and oaky winter brew, with
ripe malt, fruit cake, and sweet
sherry mystique.

### Jacobite Ale
BARLEY WINE **8%** ABV
Herbal notes from the use of coriander
warm the bittersweet chocolate and port
wine flavours.

# La Trappe

Eindhovenseweg 3, Berkel-Enschot,
**NETHERLANDS**
www.latrappe.nl

There are just seven genuine
Trappist breweries in the world;
Koningshoeven (better known as
La Trappe) is the only one outside
Belgium. The monastery had
problems recruiting new monks,
and that was one of the factors
that prompted the sale of the
brewery to Bavaria. Brewing still
takes place within the monastery
grounds under the supervision
of the monks.

### La Trappe Witte Trappist
**WITBIER 5.5% ABV**
Unspiced, but a subtle use of aromatic
hops more than compensates, providing
delicious citrus and pepper flavours.

### La Trappe Tripel
**STRONG ALE 8% ABV**
Sweetness and fruit give way to coriander,
orange, and hop bitterness in this
supremely balanced beer.

# Tsingtao

Hong Kong Road, Central,
Qinqdao, **CHINA** 266071
www.tsingtaobeer.com

The Tsingtao Brewery was
founded in 1903 by German
settlers in Qingdao. Today it is
part owned by American giants
Anheuser Busch, which is
currently undertaking a massive
investment in new breweries
on the China mainland. The
company runs over 40 breweries
and malt plants in 18 provinces
across China.

### Tsingtao

LAGER **4.8**% ABV
Crisp, slightly malty flavour and
nutty sweet taste. The colour is a bright
yellow; aroma grainy, with a hint of
sweetness. A high level of carbonation
makes it very fizzy.

# U Medvídků

Na Perštýně 7, 100 01 Prague 1,
**CZECH REPUBLIC**
www.umedvidku.cz

The restaurant and brewhouse
date back to 1466, though the
brewery has been reinstalled in
recent years – along with
extensions and additions to the
*pension*, which retains its
original Gothic rafters and
Renaissance painted ceilings.
This is one of the biggest beer
halls in Prague, and it hosted
the city's first cabaret.

### Oldgott Barique Ležák
**PILSNER 5.2% ABV**
Earthy and melon-fruity aromas, yeasty
characteristics developing into a roasted
malt, caramel infusion.

### X-Beer
**SPECIALITY BEER 12.6% ABV (VARIABLE)**
Matured for 28 weeks in oak vessels
for an elaborate, sweet flavour, and
indulgent complexity.

# Union

Pivovarniška ulica 2,
1000 Ljubljana, **SLOVENIA**
www.pivo-union.si

This brewery was founded in 1864 by the Kozler family, but state-of-the-art technology makes it one of the most modern in Slovenia. A fascinating museum takes visitors through the brewing process. However, you have to be there on the first Tuesday morning of the month to enjoy it.

### Union Lager
LAGER 5% ABV
A Slovenian favourite. A sweet, golden beer, it has corn overtones.

### ČRNI Baron / Black Baron
STOUT 5.2% ABV
A dark dessert beer, rich with caramel notes and aromas; its finish is warming but could be longer.

# United Breweries

Bengaluru, **INDIA**
www.theubgroup.com

It is said the company's logo – a Pegasus – once carried a cask of beer between its wings as gift to the gods. Its Kingfisher brand is the flying leader in India's soaring beer market, and what once was a company that supplied beer to the troops of the British Empire has now acquired a worldwide reputation.

### Kingfisher
LAGER 5% ABV
Brewed under licence in many countries. It has a crisp taste with a sweetish overtone.

### London Pilsner 5.0
LAGER 5% ABV
Thin yellow colour, some hop aroma, and a sweetish aftertaste, it smells of grass.

# Upstream

514 South 11th Street, Omaha,
Nebraska 68102, **USA**
www.upstreambrewing.com

Since opening in 1996 as part of
an "unlinked chain" started by
Wynkoop Brewery, Upstream
(a translation of the Native
American name for Omaha)
has gained independence, opened
a second pub, and brewed
varieties of beers not previously
found in Nebraska.

**BREWING SECRET** Developments
include barrel-ageing, and the use
of wild yeast.

## Batch 1000 Barley Wine
BARLEY WINE 10.2% ABV
Caramel and vinous on the nose and
palate, blending with lively fruity
esters. Rich, almost chewy, palate.

## Grand Cru
BELGIAN STRONG ALE 9% ABV
Aged for a year in oak wine barrels.
Earthy and woody nose, delicate
citrus and honey on the palate,
ultimately balanced.

# Vancouver Island

2330 Government St, Victoria,
British Colombia, V8T 5G5, **CANADA**
www.vanislandbrewery.com

The inspiration for this
company's formation in 1984 was
the absence of locally made beers
on Vancouver Island. The
brewery believes that brewing
should be a perfect blend of art
and science, with no short cuts.

**BREWING SECRET** Though the hops
and yeast are imported, only the finest
Canadian barley is used.

## Hermannator
EISBOCK **9.5% ABV**
Brewed and then frozen, it is a
symphony of complex chestnut
colours and spicy flavours.

## Hermann's Dark
BAVARIAN LAGER **5.5% ABV**
A toasty malt nose with similar flavours
on the palate; takes on a somewhat
nutty character.

# Victory

420 Acorn Lane, Downingtown,
Pennsylvania 19335, **USA**
www.victorybeer.com

Victory Brewing founders Ron
Barchet and Bill Covaleski –
who met on a school bus in
1973 – travelled much of the
beer world, apprenticed in
Germany, and worked in US
microbreweries before starting
their own in 1996. The breadth
of their interests is reflected in
the range of their beers.

**BREWING SECRET** Victory has long-
term contracts with German hop-growers
to assure the availability of authentic
ingredients for their lagers.

### Prima Pils
PILSNER 5.3% ABV
Fresh flowery aromas, cookie-like palate,
and a solidly bitter-rough finish. Sturdy
yet delicate.

### Golden Monkey
TRIPLE 9.5% ABV
Spicy, with hints of banana followed by
light pepper. Candy-sweet on the palate,
with a dry finish.

# Wadworth

Devises, Wiltshire,
SN10 1JW **ENGLAND**
www.wadworth.co.uk

Established by Henry Wadworth,
the brewery began producing
beer in 1875 and was expanded
10 years later into an impressive,
red-brick Victorian tower
brewery. The original open
copper is still operational and
wooden casks are used for local
deliveries. A full-time cooper and
a team of dray horses continue
traditional customs.

### Wadworth 6X
BEST BITTER **4.3%** ABV
A malt and fruit nose, with restrained hop
characteristics developing an intensity on
the palate.

### JEB
STRONG BITTER **4.7%** ABV
Aromatic wafts of tropical fruit; a rich
malt mouth with some nutty sweetness
on the palate.

# Weitra Bräu

Sparkassaplatz 160,
A-3970 Weitra, **AUSTRIA**
www.bierwerkstatt.at

Weitra claims to hold Austria's oldest brewing privilege, issued in 1321. In medieval times most of the buildings around the town square exercised their right to brew, now there is only one brewpub and this brewery left.

**BREWING SECRET** This organic speciality brewery, bought by Zwettler in 2002, still brews using open fermenters.

## Hadmar

ORGANIC VIENNA LAGER **5.2%** ABV
Sweet and malty on the nose and palate; hints of roatyness, bitterness; variable from batch to batch.

## Weitra Hell

LAGER **5%** ABV
Straw coloured, with estery aroma and very little carbonation. Soft on the palate, with a mild hoppyness.

# Wells & Young's

Bedford, Bedfordshire,
MK40 4LU **ENGLAND**
www.charleswells.co.uk
www.youngs.co.uk

A major force in British brewing
was created in 2006 from the
partnership of London brewer
Young's and Bedford-based
Charles Wells, two of the most
prodigiously accomplished
operators in the industry. Wells
& Young's cask and bottled ale
portfolio is one of the broadest in
the brewing sector, particularly
after Courage brands – Best Bitter
and Directors Bitter – were added
in 2007 under an agreement with
Scottish & Newcastle.

## Wells Bombardier
PREMIUM BITTER **4.3%** ABV
Powerful citrus hop aromas meet
malt and dried fruit in a richly
complex medley.

## Young's Bitter
BITTER **3.7%** ABV
Well-balanced, with citrus hop notes
and enough malt for a flowery and
bready finish.

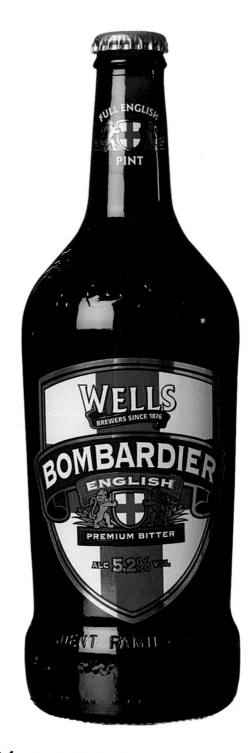

# Weltenburg

Klosterbaruerei Weltenburg,
Heitzerstr. 2, 93049 Regensburg,
**GERMANY**
www.weltenburger.de

The Benedictine abbey of
Weltenburg houses the oldest
abbey brewery in the world,
founded in 1050. The location
is delightful, close to the scenic
Donau-Durchbruch gorge.
The abbey's restaurant is famous.

**BREWING SECRET** Despite its history,
the beer is made with the most advanced
equipment, but is long-matured.

## Asam Bock
BOCK 6.9% ABV
A dark mahogany doppelbock. Very
pleasant, it tastes slightly sweet with
nice malty aromas in the finish.

## Anno 1050
EXPORT 5.5% ABV
The abbey's anniversary beer has
a distinctive mix of malt aromas
balanced with hops.

# Westmalle

Antwerpsesteenweg 496,
B2390 Malle, **BELGIUM**
www.trappistwestmalle.be

Monks started brewing here in
1836, selling beer at the gate 20
years later. Today, the abbey
operates one of the world's most
modern breweries, hidden behind
the old brewhouse. Westmalle
has come to define abbey ales
through their "Dubbel" and
"Tripel" styles. The "Extra" could
be another world classic, if the
monks were to commercialise it.

### Westmalle Dubbel

ABBEY ALE **7**% ABV
Dark and vinous, with sugar sweetness
coming through; surprisingly hoppy.
A classic.

### Westmalle Tripel

ABBEY ALE **9.5**% ABV
The dry Champenoise triple that made all
triples blond. Sweetish and fruity, with a
hoppy finish.

# Westvleteren

Donkerstraat 12,
B8640 Vleteren, **BELGIUM**
www.sintsixtus.be

The Abbey of St. Sixtus of Westvleteren is the reclusive star of the beer world. It sells its beer by telephone reservation only – unwillingly even – as if to emphasize that the operation is run by monks who brew in order to be able to pray, instead of pray in order to sell. Westvleteren voluntarily limits production.

**BREWING SECRET** This is the only remaining Trappist brewery that still employs solely in-house monks.

### Westvleteren Blond
ABBEY ALE **5.8**% ABV
A blond ale that starts with a big grain flavour, followed by very serious hops; best bitter-like.

### Westvleteren abt 12°
ABBEY ALE **10.2**% ABV
A truly massive dark Trappist ale: chewy like no other beer, and with a perfect balance between the sweet and bitter notes.

# Wickwar

Wickwar, Gloucestershire,
GL12 8NB **ENGLAND**
www.wickwarbrewing.co.uk

A million-pound refurbishment
has hoisted Wickwar from
microbrewery status to regional
heights, increasing its brewing
capacity almost fourfold. Beers
are matured in below-ground
vaults at the former Arnold
Perret & Co Brewery. The export
market is an increasing area
of interest, with encouraging
European sales.

### Station Porter
PORTER **6.1%** ABV
Richly smooth, with roast coffee,
chocolate, and dried fruits combining
with complex spiced flavours.

### IKB
BEST BITTER **4.7%** ABV
Bold in its multi-malt flavours, with rich
cherry and plum fruit breaking through.

# Widmer

929 North Russell, Portland,
Oregon 97227, **USA**
www.widmer.com

More than two decades old, the
US-centric Hefeweizen (cloudy
but accented by yeast rather than
hops) that the Widmer brothers
basically invented continues to
drive double-digit growth.
Widmer and Redhook have
merged to form a single
company called Craft Breweries
Alliance, but Widmer maintains
its own brewery.

### Hefeweizen

US HEFEWEIZEN **4.9%** ABV
Citrus, particularly lemon zest, is
matched against clean, bready-yet-tart
wheat. Finale of grapefruit.

### Snow Plow

MILK STOUT **5.5%** ABV
Coffee on the nose becomes creamier on
the palate, roasted notes blending with
rich chocolate.

# Williams

Alloa, Clackmannanshire,
FK10 1NT **SCOTLAND**
www.heatherale.co.uk

Alloa was once second only
to Burton upon Trent as a
brewing centre, so it is
encouraging to observe
innovative beer styles still
being developed there. Historic
recipes and traditional folklore
methods are skilfully applied.

**BREWING SECRET** In the Fraoch Ale,
flowering heather is used instead of hops,
reviving an ancient Celtic recipe.

### Fraoch Heather Ale

SPECIALITY BITTER **4.1%** ABV
Abundantly floral and aromatic, with
a spicy mint piquancy, malty character,
and whiff of peat.

### Kelpie Seaweed Ale

SPECIALITY BITTER **4.4%** ABV
Organic barley from coastal farms and
bladderwrack seaweed in the mash
produce beguiling flavours.

# Wismar

Kleine Hohe Str. 15, 23966 Wismar,
**GERMANY**
www.brauhaus-wismar.de

In the early 15th century there were about 180 breweries registered in Wismar, and the town was well known all over Europe. The Brauhaus Wismar was opened in 1452. Today it is the last brewery remaining in the city and, since 1995, it has brewed beer in the style of the medieval Hanseatic League breweries of northern Europe.

## Wismarer Mumme

LAGER **4.8**% ABV
An old-fashioned, golden beer with lovely aromas of malt, light hops on the tongue, and a long, sweet finish.

## Roter Eric

SPECIAL BEER **4.8**% ABV
The light red colour comes from the malt; the beer is smooth and aromatic, with a sweet finish.

# Woodforde's

Woodbastwick, Norwich, Norfolk,
NR13 6SW **ENGLAND**
www.woodfordes.co.uk

Now on its third site, the
brewery continues to increase
production capacity and to
broaden its ambitions. A
tremendous local following has
developed, and the country's top
awards have been accrued – even
for the beermats. Underpinning
all this is high-quality water,
which comes bubbling from
an on-site borehole.

### Wherry Best Bitter
BEST BITTER **3.8**% ABV
Floral and citrus fruit aromas
unlock a malt-infused middle,
then a sustained finish.

### Norfolk Nog
BITTER **4.6**% ABV
Deep red, with a roasted malt background
developing through liquorice nuances
and dried fruit.

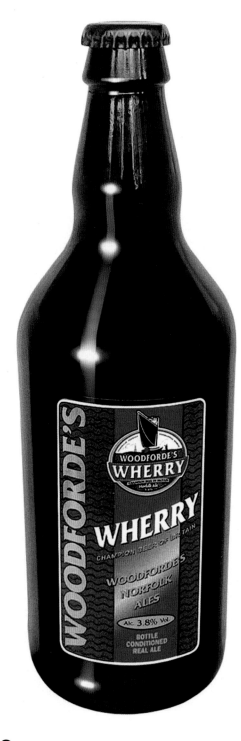

# Worthington's White Shield

Burton upon Trent, Staffordshire, DE14 1YQ **ENGLAND**
www.worthingtonswhiteshield.com

The brewery, which dates from 1920, was reopened in 1995 as a museum and in order to recreate discontinued Bass ales, which it has done successfully under head brewer Steve Wellington.

**BREWING SECRET** White Shield became a cult beer for aficionados, as it is bottled "live" and improves with age.

## White Shield

INDIA PALE ALE **5.6**% ABV
Enthusiasts appreciate its hop attack, its smokiness, treacle toffee sweetness, dusting of paprika, and serving of fried banana, stilton cheese, and sliced apple.

## Worthington Red Shield

ALE **4.2**% ABV
English and American hops - Bramling Cross, Cascade and Centennial - together with a pale malt produce a complex, satisfying beer with lots of citrus flavours.

# Yanjing

9 Shuanghe Road, Shunyi District,
Beijing, **CHINA**
www.yanjing.com.cn

The last remaining large
independent brewer in China,
Yanjing often rouses the
attention of the global brewers.
Over the past 25 years Yanjing
has developed into one of
the largest beer producing
enterprises in China. It operates
20 other breweries on the China
mainland, and its output was
predicted to reach 5 million
kiloliters (1,100 million gallons)
by 2010.

## Yanjing Beer

LAGER 5% ABV

A sweet, golden syrup nose, it has
overlays of biscuits and corn and pours
a sunburst yellow into a glass. The
brewing water is said to be from
unpolluted mineral water deep under
the Yanshan mountain.

# Yoho

1119-1 Otai, Saku City,
Nagano 385-0009, **JAPAN**
www.yonasato.com

Yona Yona Ale is perhaps the
most popular craft beer in Japan,
available in brightly coloured
cans and on draught all over
Japan. While the recipe predates
head brewer Toshi Ishii (who
previously worked at Stone
Brewing in San Diego, USA), he
is responsible for their second
big success, Tokyo Black, a tasty
porter with remarkable flavour
and smooth balance.

### Yona Yona Ale
PALE ALE 5.5% ABV
Square in the American Pale Ale category.
Brisk and citrusy, with Cascade hops
giving a sharp finish

### Tokyo Black
PORTER 5% ABV
This tasty, roasty beer can best be
described as a session porter, with
a unique twist. Brewer Ishii recently
brewed a batch in England.

# Yukon Brewing

102A Copper Rd, Whitehorse,
Yukon, Y1A 2Z6, **CANADA**
www.yukonbeer.com

Clean water makes clean beer.
Yukon beers start with North
America's cleanest water. Named
by some the Wilderness City,
Whitehorse nestles on the banks
of the famous Yukon River,
surrounded by mountains and
clear mountain lakes. Yukon
makes eight beers, including one
flavoured with coffee beans.

### Lead Dog Ale
ALE 7% ABV
Intricate malt flavours predominate.
Reminiscent of a porter, it has a slightly
darkened, creamy head.

### Discovery Ale
PALE ALE 5% ABV
Brewed using honey made from Fireweed,
the official flower of the Yukon. It finishes
dry on the tongue.

# Zagrebacka

Ilica 224, Zagreb, **CROATIA**
www.inbev.com

Zagrebacka Pivovara, Croatia's
largest brewer, was established
in 1893 and is now owned by
InBev. After years of falling
beer consumption, the market
is now growing again, with
domestic lager brands being
the most popular segment
of the market.

**BREWING SECRET** Double-malted dark
chocolate barley gives the dark lager its
prized aromas, flavours, and colour.

### Ožujsko Pivo
LAGER 5.2% ABV
A golden lager, with a deep, white head.
A sweetcorn and malt nose gives way to a
fruity finish.

### Tomislav Pivo
DARK LAGER 7% ABV
Croatia's strongest beer, this deep
ruby-red lager has aromas of roasted
malt and coffee and a dry finish.

# Žatec

Žižkovo náměstí 81, 438 01 Žatec,
**CZECH REPUBLIC**
www.zateckypivovar.cz

There is no escaping it in Czech beer production – every brewery uses the town's succulent hops, and, as far back as 1585, Žatec beer was praised for "its essence, strengths, and virtues".

**BREWING SECRET** Significant recent investment has upgraded its yeast plant, restored open fermenters, and introduced state-of-the-art kegging.

### Žatec Blue Label
PREMIUM LAGER **4.6%** ABV
Hints of grassy hop and sweet malt, then banana with biscuit malt on the palate.

### Žatec Export
PILSNER **4.6%** ABV
Bready aroma with herbal notes, some sweet malt, delicate spicy hop, and appropriate apple sourness.

# Zlatopramen

Drážďanská 80, 400 07 Ústí nad Labem, **CZECH REPUBLIC**
www.zlatopramen.cz

Modernization may have accelerated in recent years, but this brewery's history is as long as the existence of brewing privileges. The use of Austrian Emperor Franz Joseph II's eagle for its emblem was granted in the early 20th century, while the Zlatopramen trademark was adopted in 1967. It is now owned by Drinks Union.

### Zlatopramen 11°
PILSNER **4.7%** ABV
A faint, earthy hop aroma unfolds into a full biscuit flavour with a potent bitterness.

### Zlatopramen 11° Dark
DARK BEER **4.6%** ABV
Aromatically floral, its sweet palate, composed from inventive blends of barley malts, edges towards toffee.

# Zywiec

ul. Browarna 88, 34-300 Zywiec,
**POLAND**
www.zywiec.com.pl

Established in 1852 by the
Hapsburg family, this brewery
fell into state ownership after
World War II, and was acquired
by Heineken in the mid-1990s. It
is home to a lively brewing
museum that takes visitors right
through the brewing process.

**BREWING SECRET** The Zywiec Porter
uses a recipe from 1881.

## Zywiec

**LAGER 5.6% ABV**
Crisp, bright gold, and easy-drinking,
with flowery, hoppy aromas, it is now
being exported worldwide.

## Porter

**BALTIC PORTER 9.5% ABV**
A dark, strong beer, brewed with
Munich and other special malts for
sweetness and colour. Aromatic hops
provide a rich aroma.

# Index

This is an index of individual beers only, as the breweries appear in A–Z order in the book.

# Acknowledgments

**Editor-in-Chief Tim Hampson** reckons he has one of the best jobs in the world
– he is paid to drink beer for a living. A regular broadcaster and writer on
beer for many years, he has travelled the world in pursuit of the perfect drink.
Chairman of the British Guild of Beer Writers, he wants more people to
understand that beer has far greater complexity than wine can ever have. And
it is harder to make too. His work appears in *The Telegraph*, *Food & Travel*
magazine, *What's Brewing*, *Drinks International*, *Beers of the World*, *American
Brewer*, *Brewers Guardian*, and *Morning Advertiser*; he has also appeared on
BBC Good Food Live and Sky TV. He is author of *Room at the Inn*.

## Contributors
Tim Hampson • Stan Hieronymus • Werner Obalski • Joris Pattyn • Alastair
Gilmour • Lorenzo Dabove • Gilbert Delos • Conrad Sidl • Ron Pattinson •
Bryan Harrell • Willie Simpson • Geoff Griggs • Laura Stadler-Jensen • Adrian
Tierney-Jones

**The publishers would** like to thank the following people and organisations for their help
in the preparation of this book: Beers of Europe, Finn at Utobeer, Jeff at Cracked Kettle,
Lithuanian Beer, Belgian Beer Shop, The Grove Tavern, Karen Heptonstall, Malini
McCauley, Jennifer Crake at Tourmaline Editions, Florian Bucher, Dorothee Whittaker,
Tina Gehrrig, Monika Schlitzer, Ina Melzer at DK Verlag, Dirk Kaufman at DK Inc,
Rebecca Carman, Shawn Christopher, Katerina Cerna, Wojciech Kozlowski, Agnes Ordog,
Jürgen Scheunemann, Yumi Shigematsu, Diggory Williams, Nora Zimerman

## Images
The publishers would like to thank all the breweries that provided their kind assistance in
sending bottles or bottle images to be used within this book and related works.

Thank you to the following companies for their kind permission to reproduce images for
features within this book: Pelican 86 (below left); Rogue Brewery 86 (centre left)

Additional studio and location photography by Thameside Media, Quentin Bacon, Jane
Ewart, Joe Giacomet, Tim Hampson, Catherine Harries, Alex Havret, Michael Jackson ©
DK/Michael Jackson, Roger Mapp © Rough Guides, Ian O'Leary © DK, Michael
Schönwälder, Mark Thomas © Rough Guides

Maps: Casper Morris, Paul Eames, David Roberts, Iorwerth Walkins

Jacket images: (on front) Hoegaarden Wit, BridgePort India Pale Ale, Guinness Foreign
Extra Stout, Starobrno Premium Lager; (on spine) U Medvídků Oldgott Barique Ležák